Among the King's Companions

Position yourself today to be among those who reign with Christ

A Simple Study of Hebrews

Rick Oglesby

Among the King's Companions

Position yourself today to be among those who reign with Christ

Copyright © 2018 Richard Oglesby

All rights reserved.

All rights reserved solely by the author. No part of this book may be reproduced in any form without the permission of the author except in the case of brief quotations in critical articles or reviews.

Unless otherwise indicated, all Scripture quotations taken from the New American Standard Bible®(NASB), Copyright © 1960, 1962, 1963, 1968, 1971, 1972, 1973, 1975, 1977, 1995 by The Lockman Foundation. Used by permission. www.Lockman.org.

All bold emphases in quoted material are by the author unless otherwise noted.

Dedication

I gratefully dedicate this book to Bill Korver, my dear friend from our freshman year in Bible college. You are an artesian well of love, grace and generosity to me as you serve our High King. Barnabas ever comes to mind when I think of you.

To Rob Ostlund, whose unshakable love, encouragement, wisdom and reassurance walked me through my darkest days. Only you and Jesus know how. You stick closer than a brother.

And to Paul Seger, loyal friend and zealous servant leader who deeply loves those he leads. Your integrity of heart, skillfulness of hands and humility from the knees up persistently blows fresh wind into my sails.

How could God grace one man with three such companions in this life? I believe that you are a trio of the King's partners in training, and I joyfully look forward to serving you in our heavenly country. I love you.

With Gratitude

My heartfelt thanks to the faculty and staff of Southeastern Bible College in Birmingham, AL. Kinsey and I are so grateful for what you modeled, taught and did for us. Our Savior-King transformed us while with you. I pray that this book gives you pleasure from your labors.

Special thanks to Dr. James Raiford who introduced me to Hebrews in 1978. You are a priceless gift. I always recall with joy your exhortation, "Context, gentlemen, context!" Also, to Dr. John Talley whose war cry was "Anchor to the text!" Thank you, Paul Seger, for saying, "Write it." This would never have happened without you. Many thanks to Karen Keegan for her encouragement, patience and excellent work in the preparation of the manuscript. You're the best! I look forward to serving all of you when His kingdom comes.

Finally, thank you, King of kings and Lord of lords. You are my living hope.

Contents

A Word to the Reader 9

Introduction: Getting Our Bearings 11

Companions Heed the Son (1:1-2:18) 23
1. He Is God's Final Revelation (1:1-4) 25
2. He Will Rule the Angels (1:5-14) 33
3. Warning: Heed His Better Message (2:1-4) 39
4. He Restores the Kingdom (2:5-18) 45

Companions Draw Near the High Priest (3:1-10:18) 55
5. He Is a More Faithful High Priest (3:1-6) 57
6. Warning: Do Not Harden Your Heart (3:7-4:13) 63
7. He Is a Great High Priest (4:14-5:10) 75
8. Warning: Press on to Maturity (5:11-6:20) 83
9. He Is of a Better Order (7:1-28) 95

10. His Better Covenant (8:1-13) 103
11. His Better Ministries (9:1-14) 111
12. The Effects of His Better Sacrifice (9:15-10:18) 117

Companions Train to Reign with the King (10:19-13:25)............ 127
13. Warning: Be Faithful Priests (10:19-39) 129
14. Companions Seek Rewards (11:1-40) 139
15. Companions Endure Discipline (12:1-13) 153
16. Warning: Obey God's Voice (12:14-29) 163
17. Companions Serve His Priestly House (13:1-19) 173
18. Bless You! (13:20-25) 183

Appendices 189
Appendix 1. Salvation 191
Appendix 2. The Kingdom 203
Appendix 3. Rewards 209
Appendix 4. The Inheritance 225
Appendix 5. Jesus and Temptation 229
Appendix 6. The Judgment Seat 235
Appendix 7. Chastening and Pruning.. 243

A Word to the Reader

Hebrews is hard to understand. Hopefully, this commentary is not. It is not a scholarly work. Instead, it is a simple guide through Hebrews for everyday followers of Jesus.

Pastors, teachers, students and missionaries should find it helpful but it aims at the steady or struggling man and woman who follow Jesus at home and work or the believer in class or on the ballfield.

Be encouraged, be warned, be faithful. May it lift up the King and help you position yourself to be among His companions.

Introduction

Getting Our Bearings

My children and grandchildren were masters at one thing when they were small. Yours too. Asking questions: who, what, where, when, why and how. These six simple queries investigated their world and gave them their bearings.

We can head north into Hebrews seeking encouragement and guidance and quickly find ourselves west by southwest, scared and confused. The best thing to do as we enter this magnificent book is to ask some questions whose answers will help orient us to its message.

Who Wrote Hebrews?

The book has no opening address, salutation or author's name. There is no mention of the original readers and no blessing, which were usual in first century letters. In fact, Hebrews is likely a written sermon, a *word of exhortation* (13:22).

Proposals abound about the writer including Paul, Barnabas, Luke and Apollos. Whoever he was, the Hebrews knew him well (13:23). Like them, he was a second–generation Jewish believer (2:3-4).

Perhaps he wrote from Italy, and he may have been a coworker of Timothy (13:22-25).

The anonymity of the author is an encouragement. It reminds us to make Christ our focal point as he did, and that we can have a marvelous ministry even if we are largely unknown.

Who Were the Hebrews?

All we know for sure about the readers is that they were primarily Jewish believers under heavy duress.

The inclusive use of *we* and *let us* reveals an equal faith in Jesus between the author and the audience. They are *holy brethren* and *partakers of the Holy Spirit* who are *sanctified* and *enlightened*. These descriptions can only depict believers.

The author assumes their familiarity with the many Old Testament references and illustrations he uses. This, too, points to a fellowship of Jewish believers.

Where did the Hebrews live? Scholars offer many suggestions, but four seem most likely: Rome, Palestine, Jerusalem or Cyrene. There are excellent arguments and challenging problems for each. This commentary concludes that they were Jewish believers in or near Jerusalem between 66 and 69 A.D.

What Were Their Circumstances?

The troubled Hebrews struggled daily to pay the steep price of faithfulness to Jesus. Wounds from past abuse, imprisonment and loss of property for their faith were still raw (10:32–39). Now they were looking at possible martyrdom (12:4).

Additionally, if a destination of Jerusalem is correct, tensions with Rome were rising. The acrid smell of smoldering rebellion influenced all of Palestine.

In 66 A.D. the Roman procurator Florus seized silver from the temple to cover low tax revenues. A quick and immense uproar followed and Florus sent troops into Jerusalem to stop it. His soldiers massacred 3,600 Jews which touched off an explosive rebellion. The revolt then moved from Masada to Judea and on to Galilee. Around four years later on August 3, 70 A.D., the future emperor Titus recaptured and devastated Jerusalem and destroyed the temple. Josephus claims that 1.1 million people were killed during the siege and 97,000 were enslaved.[1]

Deeply wearied by their weighty apprehensions and troubles, some brothers looked for a way out. The simplest choice was to return to temple worship. Why not? What harm could come of a periodic sacrifice? Like us, their most essential needs were faithfulness and perseverance.

What Are Some of the Big Ideas?

We approach our Bibles with Reformation and Puritan presuppositions. But first-century Christians read their Bible, primarily the Old Testament, through Jesus and Jewish bifocals. We must try to do likewise to hear what they heard. Consider several essential concepts in Hebrews from their context.

Exposition of the Old Testament

The author anchored his letter firmly to the text of the Old Testament. He quotes, alludes to, explains or applies over 80 Greek Old Testament passages to make two primary points. First, Jesus is absolutely superior to old covenant Judaism. Then, endurance is necessary for eternal inheritance and rewards.

To spotlight Jesus' person and work over the old covenant system, the writer employs the word *better* 13 times and the term *perfect* 14 times. Using the Law, the Psalms, and the Prophets he proves Jesus is the promised King–Priest–Son. There is no comparison. Jesus is greater.

Hebrews is a potent reminder to become more familiar with the first half of our Bible.

Salvation

We tend to hear Hebrews through earbuds of "salvation means saved from hell to go to heaven" and "behavior proves belief." But Hebrews differs.

Salvation is both a rescue and a restoration, a deliverance from a state of brokenness to one of wholeness. In either Testament, that change might be from any number of things such as danger to safety (Ex 14:30; Mt 14:30) or from troubles to tranquility (Pr 34:6; Mt 14:30-32). There is rescue from illness to health (Ps 103:3; Mt 9:22) and from enemies to peace (Ps 18:3; Lk 1:71).

Old Testament salvation rarely refers to "getting saved." It usually means release from the struggles with temporal life or enemies into peace. Often it is deliverance from God's temporal wrath into covenant fellowship. And over and again it speaks of rescue from this world into the coming kingdom.

Reflecting this, salvation in Hebrews is almost wholly a future event as in Romans 13:11. It is liberty from the challenges of following Jesus in this life into the life of rest and rewards in the millennium.

This kingdom salvation stands behind the consistent appeals to endure. Perseverance is not urged to prove the reality of faith but to gain the kingdom rewards of faith (1:14; 2:3, 10; 5:9; 6:9; 9:28; 11:6-7). Failure to continue following Jesus loses rewards but not eternal life. Eternal life depends on God's faithfulness to His word and Himself (Jn 3:16; 5:24; 11:25-26). Rewards depend on our allegiance to Him. See Appendix 1.

The Kingdom

Genesis reveals that in the beginning God crafted Adam and Eve for three roles. As His image they were made to fellowship with

Him and others; to follow or obey His command and to rule as servant kings of the earth (Gn 1:26-31; 2:15–17). Adam's sin derailed all three, but in the end, God saves. Revelation 22:3-5 says that *His bondservants will serve Him*—followership; *they will see His face and His name will be on their foreheads*—fellowship, *and they shall reign forever and ever*—rulership.

To vindicate His sovereignty, God will restore (save) His earthly dominion and believers will enjoy all for which He made us. His kingdom and His saving Son--King are the threads that tie Scripture together.

Hebrews points us to the millennium—*the world* [Gk. inhabited earth] *to come* (2:5) and its promised rewards as a prime motivation to faithful endurance. See Appendix 2.

Rewards

The Old Testament doctrine of rewards for righteousness and faithfulness rolls through Hebrews in ten of thirteen chapters (Gn 15:1; Ru 2:12; Pr 13:13; Is 40:10, et al.).

Take chapter eleven, a record of Old Testament believers who sought God and His rewards. They believed that He wants to reward those who seek Him (11:6, 24–26, 35).

That belief molded their worldview, values and choices. It empowered them to trek as aliens through this world for recompense in the future one. The author encourages the readers to do likewise. See Appendix 3.

Companions, Partners or Partakers

Companionship or partnership or being a *partaker* with Christ is an exclusive reward, and Hebrews is the only place the Bible refers to it. The Greek words *metochos* ("meh–tah–kos") or *metochoi* ("meh–tah–koi" plural) translate as *partakers*, *partners* or *companions*. It describes those who participate in the same business, event or experience. This term appears six times in the New Testament--five in Hebrews. Luke 5:7 is the lone other use. There it describes Simon, James and John as business partners and friends working their fishing business together.

Companions or *partakers* designates believers who will share a singular role with the King forever (1:9). They seem to be special friends and servants who share in His unique kingly joy (1:9). Perhaps they will assist on His ruling council (1:9) as His business partners (3:14; Lk 5:7). Joseph Dillow refers to them as "servant kings."[2]

Companions will ever know Jesus more intimately. They will appreciate His desires and pleasures better then because they do so now. Such honored servants will play more significant roles than others throughout eternity. Perhaps they will be somewhat like David's mighty men.

God desires that His Son have as many faithful companions and coworkers as possible. So, Hebrews reminds us that today's decisions and activities fix our kingdom roles based on the quality of our Christian life.

Inheritance

Christians hold two inheritances. One is a gift received at the moment of belief in Christ. We are **unconditionally** made heirs of God forever by grace through faith in Christ (Gl 3:23; 4:6-7; Rm 8:17a; Ti 3:4-7). We do nothing to gain it and possess it now and forever. This inheritance cannot be changed, lessened or lost. It is staggering what it includes. See Appendix 4.

Our second inheritance is the *reward of the inheritance* or to *inherit the kingdom*. It is **a conditional eternal reward** for good works now. We will receive it at the judgment seat. Those who persevere in fellowship, obedience, service and suffering will gain it. If we do not, we can lose or lessen it.

Don't confuse the two. We receive eternal life and enter the kingdom by grace alone through belief alone in Jesus alone (Jn 3:3,

5). We become God's heirs at that instant (Ti 3:3-7). However, to *inherit the kingdom* does not mean to get saved or to go to heaven. It means to obtain one's second inheritance by works as a reward (1 Cr 6:9-11; Gl 5:19-21; Ep 5:3-5; Co 3:22-25; 2 Tm 2:12, et al.).

Our Savior-King will inherit rule of all things as a reward for His faithful obedience (1:4-9; 2:5-18; 12:2). Only those who, like Him, persevere in righteousness will gain their full inheritance. All believers will be in the kingdom and can earn rewards, but only some will attain full inheritance; that demands more.

A new President appoints a cabinet shortly after his election to help him govern. His partners are often faithful supporters who have worked hard to promote him by giving, planning, serving and sacrificing. Most of all they have demonstrated unfaltering loyalty and faithfulness. The President will govern all citizens, but they will not function as his cabinet companions. He reserves that privilege for those whom he appointed as a reward for their faithfulness.[3]

Position

The author often employs the theological concept of position and practice. Position is an unchanging legal or functional standing that God assigns to a nation, a people group or a person. Practice is the application of that position in day-to-day life.

The New Testament tells us that God made believers in Jesus legally holy by position in Christ. We are saints. At the same time, Peter commands us to be holy—that is our practice.

Position is like citizenship, except that you cannot lose it or give it up. You legally possess all the rights, privileges and responsibilities of citizenship through birth. What you do with your citizenship is your practice. You may or may not choose to vote, own property, serve on a jury, etc. But, whether you act on your legal standing or not, your position is unchangingly that of a citizen.

Our Position in Christ	Our Practice in Christ
Is Legal	Is Experiential
Relates to our standing before God	Relates to our walk before men
We are holy from God's perspective	We are becoming holy in practice
God's instantaneous work	God's progressive work
Occurs instantly at salvation	Occurs progressively in our life
A result of our faith in Christ	A result of our faith and obedience
Is complete, perfect and unchanging	Is incomplete, imperfect and variable
Is the same for every believer	Varies with each saint each moment
Is a basis for our growth	Is the progress of our growth

The meaning of terms in Hebrews like *sanctified, perfect, cleansed, house* and *partaker* all depend on the difference between position and practice.

House

God decreed that Levi was the priestly tribe, so priests could never be kings. Judah was the royal tribe, but no one from Judah could be a priest. Thus, Israel could never have a king-priest.

Even though He is from Judah, Jesus' resurrection and ascension made Him King-Priest. By grace, He made all believers His royal priesthood, a priestly *house* (1 Pt 2:5, 9; Hb 3:6; 10:21; Rv 1:4–6). The concept of community life as priests weaves throughout Hebrews. Responsiveness to the Lord and our brothers is a trait of faithfulness.

Trustworthy priests cling to Christ and the fellowship and witness until death or the Rapture (3:6). As fellow priests we stir one another to faithfulness (3:12-13) and train to reign together (12:1-11;

13:13-14). We promote holiness and endurance in one other (10:19-25; 12:12-17) and serve God and others together (13:15-16).

Exhortations to Endurance

The writer employs five admonitions to motivate the readers. Each uses an Old Testament event for a stern caution as well as positive inspiration. Their steady pulse is to faithfully hear and heed God's word to escape His temporal wrath and gain eternal reward.

Background of the Warnings in Hebrews		
Warning	**Old Testament Event**	**Old Testament Passage**
Drifting	Giving the Law at Sinai	Dt 33:1-5; Ac 7:53;
Disbelief	Wilderness rebellion	Nm 13-14; Ps 95
Dullness	Promise to Abraham	Gn 22:17-18
Desertion	Korah's rebellion	Nm 16:32-38; 26:10
Denying	Receiving the Law at Sinai	Ex 19:9-23; Dt 5:22-27
Hear and heed God's Word		

- *Drifting* from Jesus' kingdom message (2:1-4)

Companions must more earnestly heed the kingdom word.

- *Disbelieving* Jesus' promises about kingdom rest (3:7-4:13)

Companions must believe and work to inherit kingdom rest.

- *Dullness* in applying Jesus' kingdom truths (5:11-6:20)

Companions must apply kingdom truth to inherit its promises.

- *Deserting* Jesus' priestly house and kingdom prep (10:19-39)

Companions must continue to function as His priestly house.

- *Denying* Jesus' kingdom word and work (12:14-29)

Companions must hear, heed and reverence the King.

The several possible understandings of the cautions have many nuances. This commentary does not discuss the various views other than here. No misrepresentation is intended below.

Interpreting the Warnings in Hebrews		
Calvinist	Arminian	Companion
To lost/ professors	To believers	To believers
Get saved	Don't neglect salvation	Temporal judgment
Hell awaits	May lose salvation	May miss inheritance
Get saved	Will lose salvation	May be unable to grow
Get saved	Don't lose salvation	God's reprisal possible
God condemns	God condemns	May miss inheritance

This commentary reflects the author's companion interpretation. They are real warnings that speak to believers about losing rewards. They do not address unbelievers or false professors, nor do they threaten sinning believers with loss of salvation.

The Theme of Hebrews

Some persecuted Jewish believers were considering a return to Judaism. In response, the author presents Jesus as God's King-Priest-Son. He is superior to all of Judaism in person, purpose, priesthood and promise. When He brings His kingdom, He will reward those who endure until death or the Rapture.

Reverting to Judaism may release much of the Hebrews' pressures. Still, it would be an act of disbelieving, deliberate falling away or apostasy from King Jesus. To do so would bring God's temporal wrath and could cost the deserter his or her kingdom roles and rewards.

The author combats that temptation by urging them to:

- Embrace Jesus' supremacy as God's King-Priest-Son.
- Endure trials by persevering faith in God's rewards.
- Encourage one another to pursue companionship.

The theme is: Eternal companionship with King Jesus is a reward for active faith that endures until death or the Rapture.

Positioning for Companionship

Now that we have a sense of direction, let's apply. Partnership is gained or lost in this life, so now is the time to position ourselves for it. We have no guarantee of tomorrow. Hebrews calls this brief opportunity *Today* (3:7, 13, 15; 4:7).

Team up with another person or two to work through the questions. The shared experience will aid your growth as a priest and help you get to one another more closely. Think carefully and answer honestly.

1. Do I want to be among the King's companions? Why or why not?

2. You need a companion(s) to prepare to partner. Who will you recruit to walk with you through this study of Hebrews?

3. When will you contact him or her? To whom will you report that you have done so? When will you report?

4. What is your major take–away from this introduction?

---

[1] Flavius Josephus and William Whiston, *The Works of Josephus: Complete and Unabridged* (Philadelphia: John C. Winston, 1957), 832.

[2] Joseph Dillow, *The Reign of the Servant Kings* (Miami Springs, FL: Schoettle Publishing Co., 1992).

[3] Ray Baughman, *The Kingdom of God Visualized* (Chicago: Moody Press, 1972), 7.

Section 1

Companions Heed the King-Priest-Son
1:1-2:18

In 1:1-2:18, the author introduces God's King–Priest–Son. The Son is God's ultimate word to man. As King He will restore, inherit and rule the world to come. As Priest, He has purified believers of their sins and leads them along the path to partnership. The writer presents His greatness to encourage the readers to heed His word and endure their sufferings to co-rule as His companions.

Chapter 1

He Is God's Final Revelation
(1:1-4)

Sir Winston Churchill reportedly said,

> If you have an important point to make, don't try to be subtle or clever. Use a pile driver. Hit the point once. Then come back and hit it again. Then hit it a third time—a tremendous whack.[1]

Our author pummeled his opening 17 times in 4 verses. Eight names, nouns or pronouns and nine deeds exalt God's Son as His last and best word to man.

God spoke to Israel for over 14 centuries through His prophets. They were cherished, significant men and heroes to many Jewish persons. But the sermon opens with the proposition that God gave a better revelation. Without denigrating them whatsoever, our author demonstrates that the Son is far, far superior to the prophets. How?

He Revealed a Better Message (1:1-2a)

(1) *God, after he spoke long ago to the fathers in the prophets in many portions and in many ways in these last days has spoken to us in His Son.*

In the past the prophets repeatedly called Israel to covenant faithfulness and promised a glorious kingdom. They spoke God's word in *many portions*, a little here, a little there.

God also spoke *in many ways* to soften hard hearts, to hold Israel's attention and to make His revelation memorable.

Some Ways God Spoke Creatively Through the Prophets	
In Visions	To Abraham, Moses and Daniel (Gn 15:1; Nm 12:6; Dn 7:1)
In Dreams	To Jacob, Moses and Daniel (Gn 28:12-13; Nm 12:6; Dn 7:1)
By Angels	To Abraham and Daniel (Gn 22:11, 15; Dn 8:13)
In Events	To Moses (Ex 3:2)
Face to Face	To Moses (Nm 12:8)
In Whispers	To Elijah (1 Kg 19:11-13)

Always progressive, partial and incomplete, the prophets disclosures were various colors on the palette, but never the finished masterpiece. They were good, but the Son was better because the many incomplete messages of the Old Testament pointed to, merged and concluded in Him.

(2a) However, *in these last days God has spoken to us in Son.* The *last days* designate the time of Messiah's coming (8:6, 10). He would arrive to judge and redeem Israel, mediate the new covenant, destroy Israel's enemies and usher in the kingdom (Is 2:1-4; Ek 38:16; Hs 3:5; Mc 4:1; Jl 2:28-32).

The term *these* reminded the readers that now the new covenant was in operation. The old was finished and the kingdom was imminent—a new age had begun when the Son appeared and spoke. He closed the curtain on the age of the prophets and entered the final act, where we also play our parts.

What God announced through the prophets was initial and vital. What He spoke through His Son was final and superior.

The Son Spoke Better Than the Prophets (1:1-2)	
The Prophets	**The Son**
After He spoke (1a)	He has spoken (2b)
Long ago (1b)	In these last days (2a)
To the fathers (1c)	To us (2c)
In the prophets (1d)	In Son (2d)
In many portions & ways (1e)	In one final Person (2d)
Partial and Predictive	**Final and Fulfillment**

The Son as God's final revelation does not deny the disclosure of the rest of the New Testament. In fact, it makes it possible.

The Son's Revelation of the New Testament		
Began	In His words and works (Jn 14:9-11)	Eyewitnesses saw and heard Him (Hb 2:3-4)
Continued	In His revelation to the apostles (Jn 16:12-15)	Apostles received His word (Ac 1:1-2; Rv 1:1)
Ended	By His inspiration of the words (2 Tm 3:16-17)	Apostles recorded His word (Jd 1:3; Rv 22:6-7)
God has spoken in Son and finished what He had to say.		

He Is the Better Messenger (1:2b-4)

(2) Not only does *His Son* bring a better message, He **is** a better messenger. His person is higher than the prophets. The NASB translators supplied *His*, whereas the Greek phrase is *in* Son. The lack of the Greek pronoun or article stresses His uniqueness.

Son certainly includes deity but here it is a technical title for "God's King," the promised Son of David who will rule the world (Ps 2:17).

Seven phrases capture His overwhelmingly superior person.

He Is Heir of All Things (2b)

(2b) The Son is the one *whom He appointed heir of all things*. This is the first mention of *heir* or inheritance. The firstborn son in a Jewish family received twice the inheritance from his father. In a royal family, the heritage often involved the succession of the kingdom to the king's son.

Here, the Father allotted the Son future rule over all things—not just Israel or the earth, but all things! He presently holds all authority (Mt 28:18) but does not yet exercise it as King directly on earth (1 Cr 15:22-28; Ph 2:9-11). He will receive His earthly inheritance at the second coming.

He Made the Ages (2c)

(2c) *Through whom also He made the world* [Gk. ages]. He certainly made the universe, but the emphasis is that He made and directs creation through the ages to bring His kingdom. The Son created and controlled the eras in which the prophets simply served.

He Is the Radiance of God's Glory (3a)

(3a) When you are outside on a bright day, you do not look directly at the sun. Instead, you see its light, its radiance. Likewise, to see the Son, *the radiance of His glory*, is to see the full perfection of God in human flesh (Ex 33:18-34:9; Jn 1:14-18). No one could see God under the old covenant, not even Moses the greatest prophet. But to see the Son was to see God's glory in the flesh so He is even more significant than the ultimate prophet, the Lawgiver.

He Reveals God's Nature (3b)

(3b) He is also *the exact representation of His nature.* The term *representation* described the imprint of a signet ring on wax.[2] When you saw the imprint, you saw a precise likeness of the signet. Jesus is God. When He talked, ate, drank, paid taxes, went to a wedding, healed and listened, His words and works perfectly unveiled who God is and what He is like, especially in relationship to people (Jn 14:9-10; 1 Jn 1:1-3).

If you want to get to know the Father better, then read the life of Christ in the Gospels. Listen to His words and meditate on His works. You'll find the Father in Him.

He Upholds All Things (3c)

(3c) *He upholds* [Gk. carries forward] *all things by the word of His power* (Co 1:17). The Son holds the universe together while He conveys it toward His kingdom. As God the Creator He made, sustains and directs everything by His word.

This would have been a great comfort to the hurting Hebrews. It's fabulous to realize that the Son made yesterday, today and all our tomorrows. He drives all our circumstances to His appointed end. We may not see or sense it, but His hand is indeed on the wheel of our life. Let Him uphold you in your weaknesses and sufferings as the author challenged the Hebrews to do.

He Made Purification of Sins (3b)

(3d) *When He had made purification of sins* is the first mention of the Son as God's priest and implies the new covenant, the subjects that will consume chapters 3-10. All prophets needed cleansing, and the Son–King–Priest provided it by His sacrifice and resurrection. The Greek grammar indicates that the purging is complete and that He accomplished it by Himself of His own choice. There is no need whatsoever to return to insufficient and repeated animal sacrifices.

He Sits at the Right Hand of God (3e-4)

(3e-4) The Son *sat down at the right hand of the Majesty on high* as anointed King-Priest for His sacrificial work was done (Ps 110:4).

This is not the earthly throne in Jerusalem promised to David's son. The Son will sit there in the millennium (2 Sm 7:14; Is 9:6-7; Dn 7:13-14; Lk 1:32-33). He now rules the church and the angelic host from God's right hand (Ep 1:18-23; Co 1:18; 2:10).[3]

He sat down *having become as much better than the angels as He has inherited a more excellent name than they.* He inherited the name *Son* which includes His positions as Priest–King. He is indeed better than the prophets and their revelation, and so all of Judaism. This is the first of 13 uses of the word *better* (6:9; 7:7, 19, 22; 8:6 [twice]; 9:23; 10:34; 11:16, 35, 40; 12:24) in contrast to Judaism.

The Son Is a Superior Person to the Prophets (1:2b-4)	
The Son Is	**The Prophets Are**
Inheritor and Creator of all	Creatures who may inherit some
Reflector and Revealer of God	Receivers and recorders for God
Sustainer of all	Followers sustained by the Son
Redeemer and Ruler	In need of a redeemer and ruler
God Has Spoken in Son	

The author has laid the foundation for the remainder of his letter. The prophets **spoke** God's word whereas the Son **is** God's final word and therefore superior in the message and as the messenger.

Positioning for Companionship

1. Share your major take–away from this chapter with your companion.

2. We dare not overlook the Old Testament. Read Psalm 2 several times this week. Record every stated or implied mention of Jesus and His kingdom that you find. Check New Testament cross references. Share your discoveries with your friend. Discuss how His greatness and empire affects the direction of your life.

3. As a result of this chapter and our discussion I will:

4. I will start on the following date:

---

[1] Attributed to Winston Churchill but no historical documentation.

[2] William Barclay, *The Letter to the Hebrews*, The Daily Study Bible (Philadelphia: Westminster Press, 1976), 14.

[3] Thomas L. Constable, "Notes on Hebrews" (2015): 15.

Chapter 2

He Will Rule the Angels
(1:5-14)

One afternoon our family met a potential buyer of some property we had on the market. "What peaked your interest in our lot?" I asked. "Oh, my angel told me to buy it" she gushed.

That began an interesting conversation about her relationship with angels. She'd built her belief system on personal experience, Shirley McClain, a couple of television shows and talks with friends. Her view of angels truly impacted her life.

Angels were a pillar in Judaism, too, and the Bible has much to say about them. Among many other activities, they celebrated at creation (Jb 38:7), rescued the righteous (Gn 19), wrestled fallen angels (Dn 10) and conveyed God's messages to men (Dn 8-12). Indeed, the term *angel* means, "messenger" which was their primary ministry. Most notably, at least 10,000 angels mediated the Law from God to Moses (Dt 33:2; Ac 7:53; Gl 3:19; Hb 2:2).

Though angels were a mainstay of Judaism, neither they nor their revelation can compare to the Son. He is supreme in person, dignity, authority, and roles. He is a better word than those brought by either prophets or angels.

Seven observations demonstrated the Son's superiority to the prophets in 1:1-4. Now the writer quotes seven Old Testament passages to validate His supremacy over angels. The two sets of seven probably attest completion and aid memorization, as does the structure of the paragraph.[1]

Two phrases encase His preeminence: *to which of the angels did He ever say* (5) and *to which of the angels has He ever said* (13). The quotes, six from the Psalms and one likely from 2 Samuel, demonstrate that the Son is better than angels because He is the God–Man who will fulfill God's covenant with David and rule earth forever.

He Has a Better Name (1:4-5a)

(4) The Son is superior to the angels because *He has inherited a more excellent name than they*. One's name in the ancient world often described his or her character. No angel ever received the name Son of God, nor does Scripture ever designate an angel "the" son of God. Angels are sons of God collectively, created as servants (Jb 1:6; 2:1; 38:7). On the other hand, Jesus is His uncreated individual Son.

(5a) He is also God's royal Son, the One who will reign and rule. The question, *For to which of the angels did He ever say, "You are My Son?"* demands a negative answer. This quote from Psalm 2:7 looks ahead to the day the Son will occupy David's throne and rule all nations, which no angel can do.

In Old Testament cultures, a king was "begotten" or "born" on the day he succeeded to the throne. God declared Jesus' "birth" as Son-Priest-King after His ascension (Ps 2:7-9; Ac 13:33). The angels have no such name, for they have no such position.

The Son is not yet on David's throne for that will be on earth in Jerusalem in the millennium. He currently sits beside the Father on His priestly throne, waiting to return and rule the earth.

He Is David's Promised Son (1:5b)
(5b) *I will be a Father to Him and He shall be a Son to Me* likely quotes 2 Sm 7:14 or, perhaps, 1 Ch 17:13. It, too, is part of God's covenant with David that He will fulfill.

Jesus has always been God's Son, but when He stepped into time, He became David's human descendant and God's human Son, able to redeem and rule (Lk 1:32-33). Thus, He is far greater than the angels.

He Is the Returning Firstborn (1:6)
(6) *And when He again brings the firstborn into the world, He says, "And let all the angels of God worship Him."* In this quote of Psalm of 97:7, *again* refers to the second coming. Angels will worship Him at His return just as they celebrated Him at His first coming. He is better.

When He returns it will be as *firstborn*. This doesn't always mean born first but rather the son who is positioned as first in honor and preeminence in a family. The firstborn son functioned as family priest, shared the father's authority, received a special blessing and inherited a larger share of the father's property. In royal families, the firstborn succeeded to the throne. As God's firstborn, the Son has priority of rank over all things, including the angels.

Use of the term *world* is significant. It was the term that described the Roman Empire, meaning the "inhabited earth." In Judaism it was a technical term for Messiah's coming kingdom and is used that way in Hebrews 2:5. When the *firstborn* returns, the angels will *worship Him* as King for He is superior in person, rank and role.

He Is the Sovereign Creator (1:7)
(7) The Son fashioned the angels as His servants, variable in form and function according to Psalm 104:4, for *of the angels He says, "Who makes His angels winds, and His ministers a flame of fire."* Angels are as powerful and quick and changing as wind and fire, but they are

creatures. They are His messengers and ministers, while the Son is their unchanging Creator-King.

He Is the God-Man-King (1:8-9)

(8) In contrast to the changing angels, *of the Son He says, "Your throne, O God, is forever and ever, and the righteous scepter is the scepter of His kingdom."* Amazingly, in Psalm 45:6-7, God addresses the Son as God! He is both God and distinct from God. As God, His throne is everlasting and His rule is righteous.

(9) Now the author describes the Son's human life and ensuing millennial rule. *You have loved righteousness and hated lawlessness. Therefore God, Your God, has anointed You with the oil of gladness above Your companions* (Ps 45:6-7). On His return to heaven, God anointed the Son to celebrate His perfect human righteousness while living in an unrighteous place.

Companions could be angels but that is doubtful. Companionship is a reward for those who, like the King, choose righteousness, faithfully serve and endure difficulties. Elect angels can only choose to serve—they have no other option. Additionally, Hebrews uses *metochoi* exclusively to speak of believers (3:1, 14; 6:4; 12:8). If correct, it seems likely the psalm speaks prophetically of believers who will be His future celebratory partners in rule.

The King–Son will form His cadre of comrades from those who also love righteousness. He will ever be the focus, but His companions will enjoy eternal recognition, identification and association as His partners.

He Is the Immutable Creator (1:10-12)

(10-12) Psalm 102:25-27 declares that *You,* **LORD** [Yahweh of the Old Testament; cf. Jn 12:37-41] *in the beginning laid the foundation of the earth.* At that time, the angels celebrated Him as Creator (Jb 38:7).

But creation is aging, and He will replace it like discarded old clothes, for *like a garment they will also be changed.* In contrast, He neither ages nor changes: *But You are the same, and Your years will not come to an end*. The immutable, eternal Creator-King will remake this universe and rule the new one forever. Angels can only cover their faces before Him.

He Is the Waiting Victor (1:13-14)

(13) To ratchet down his Biblical argument for the superiority of the Son to angels, the author closes the section with a final declaration from God in Psalm 110:1: *but to which of the angels has He ever said, "Sit at My right hand, until I make Your enemies a footstool for Your feet?"* Christ will not return and take up His thousand year rule until the Father humbles His defeated enemies under the Son's feet.

After the millennium, with all physical and spiritual foes defeated (1 Cr 15:24-26; Rv 20:14), the Son will sit beside the Father and rule the new universe forever (Rv 22:1-5). No angel has ever heard such a charge.

(14) The writer sums up the angels' role with a question. *Are they not all ministering spirits, sent out to render service for the sake of those who will inherit salvation?* In this context, *inherit salvation* is future rescue from all enemies to an inheritance in His kingdom.

We can draw comfort and confidence that our walk to the kingdom has unseen aides. The visible world is a beautiful but fearful, fallen place while the invisible realm is occupied with those hostile to Christ and His own. Thankfully, God wants to give us to His Son as companions, so He assigns elect angels to assist us.

They protect us physically, wrestle enemy spirits who attack us, and it is possible angels may visit and encourage us from time to time. They are our unknown assistants who labor at the king's word to see that we have needed help to faithfully persevere. We are not alone in our struggles at any time or in any circumstance.

Nature	The Son Has a More Excellent Name than the Angels (1:4-14)			
	The Son	The Angels	Verses
Position	The Firstborn Son-King	Servant Worshippers	(5-6)
Person	The Unchanging God	Changing Ministers	(7-9)
Practice	The Creator-Victor	Subject Creatures	(10-14)

Seven proofs from Psalms and 2 Samuel demonstrate the superiority of the King–Son to the angels. Angels can never share His dignity and authority. This means that His word is also better than the Law which angels brought from God to the people. That will be the author's next topic.

Positioning for Companionship

1. Share your major take–away from this chapter with your companion.

2. Discuss an event or scenario with your friend where your angel may have assisted you.

3. As a result of this chapter and our discussion I will:

4. I will start on the following date:

---

[1] Thomas L. Constable, "Notes on Hebrews" (2015): 18.

Chapter 3

Heed
His Better Message
(2:1-4)

Scott Baldwin, who plays professional rugby for the Welsh Ospreys, was in South Africa for a game against South African franchise Cheetahs. He was visiting the Bloemfontein Zoo prior to the game and was caught on camera stretching his arms between the bars of a cage in an attempt to stroke three big cats as they grazed in the sun.

The rugby ace immediately regretted his decision after one of the lions was seen suddenly turning its head and clamping its jaws around Scott.

Dramatic video footage shows the men beginning to scream and running backwards before sighing with relief when Scott manages to escape. The 29-year-old was taken to hospital where he received stitches and treatment to prevent infection.

The incident left the player fearing he would lose both his hand and his career after an infection began to spread up his arm. "I had two operations in South Africa, flew home with an IV drip in my arm and then had another two at home. At one stage I was told I would need plastic surgery and could lose my left hand."[1]

Yet his coach, Steve Tandy, didn't have any sympathy for his player, saying Scott had ignored instructions not to pet the animal. "It was a good environment and we were told how far back to stand."[2]

The cost for failing to heed a warning can be exceedingly high.

This is the first of the five cautions. Each is rather like a "So what?" that interrupts the flow of thought to pointedly apply the preceding section. This warning exhorts the readers to *pay much closer attention to what we have heard.* Since the Son—Priest—King is greater than the angels, we should take the revelation that came through Him more seriously. The author gives four reasons to heed it far more carefully.

Because of the Son's Great Person (2:1a)

(1a) *For this reason,* since the Son is greater than the prophets and angels and their messages, the Hebrews *must pay much closer attention* to His kingdom word. Jesus began His ministry speaking of His future dominion (Mt 4:17) and ended it the same way, teaching the apostles about it for His last forty days on earth (Ac 1:3). One does not wisely ignore the passion and purpose of the majestic Son–King.

Because of the Great Peril (2:1b)

(1b) Close attention to kingdom truth is non-optional for those who would be companions: *we **must** pay much closer attention to what we have heard.* The Greek term for *closer attention* is significant. To ancient seamen it meant to watch closely in order to carefully steer the ship to the dock without hitting or missing it. To peer intently into the kingdom and its rewards and to navigate our life by them both protects us and prepares us for it.

If we neglect the kingdom, **we** slip away from its rewards; **we** are the ones who suffer. *Drift away* translates another nautical term that pictures an unanchored ship slowly floating into danger unnoticed because no one is paying attention. The hazard is to be caught up by the currents or waves and dashed into the rocks. Some of the Jewish believers were slowly drifting back into Judaism where God's judgment could sink them. Like them, we must realize that the message doesn't drift, we do!

Because of the Great Penalty (2:2-3a)

(2-3a) The writer argues from lesser to greater to explain the penalty of neglect. Disobeying *the word spoken through angels* (the lesser Law) incurred an *unalterable* and *just penalty* for *every transgression* and *disobedience*. The Law prescribed severe consequences for deliberate sin, including death for apostasy. How much greater then will our accountability be *if we neglect so great a salvation*. This equates indifference to the kingdom to a high-handed sin against the King.

So great a salvation does not refer to forgiveness of sins and eternal life. It is the same *salvation* as in 1:14 about believers' possible kingdom inheritance. This is clear, for the first chapter concerns the Son's role as King and the author tells us in 2:5 that he is speaking of *the world to come*. In addition, he includes himself in the warning six times (*we, us*).

Only a believer can neglect salvation (growth, seeking rewards, etc.). No unbeliever neglects believing in Jesus; he or she rejects Him.

Relating that God will judge us in the present if we fail to closely heed His word also reminds the reader of another truth. Interestingly, the author used a specific expression to arrest the Hebrews' hearts. The Greek term translated *just penalty* is one of the words for reward. You could read it as "fair wage" or "just reward." He is also telling the readers that there are two classes of kingdom rewards: rewards gained and rewards lost.

The author does not say what the just penalty for *neglect* might be; he simply leaves us to ponder the unknown danger. The just rewards inflicted under the Law were spiritual and temporal, sometimes including loss of inheritance and/or death. If we disregard *so great salvation*, we cannot escape the severe results that will come. Indifference will result in unspecified results. Whatever the payback, it will be right.

Because of the Great Proofs (2:3b-4)

(3b-4) Believers must also heed the kingdom disclosure because of how God validated it. *It was at the first spoken through the Lord*; then, eyewitnesses and apostles, *those who heard*, accurately broadcast His message to others. Finally, the apostles, *God also testifying with them*, verified Christ's teaching *by signs and wonders and by various miracles and by gifts of the Holy Spirit* (2 Cr 12:12). When the writer sent this letter, the apostles were no longer present and their incredible works had ceased, but their validation of the message remained in force.

The Law ordered two or three attesting witnesses; the better kingdom message has five: Jesus, the eyewitnesses, the apostles' miracles, God and the Holy Spirit. All readers can be encouraged that the kingdom message was absolutely verified and trustworthy. At the same time, so many witnesses permanently assure its paramount importance to God and the great dangers in drifting away.

We dare not neglect such profound proof of our *so great salvation* message. We must hear the King's Kingdom word and heed it. We make decisions, witness, serve, use resources, relate to others and respond to suffering with eyes fixed on the kingdom. Our responses will decide our eternal roles. If we heed the message, we will prosper when we get there. Should we neglect it, we will drift away now. When we drift, God may judge us now and we will definitely lose some eternal benefits.

Yogi Berra once said as astutely as ever, "When you come to a fork in the road, take it!" Adhere to the message now and we never need to suffer the sore back and blistered hands of coming back. It's easy to drift downstream—all we must do is nothing; the hard work is turning around and rowing back against the current.

Positioning for Companionship

1. Share your major take–away from this chapter with your brother or sister.

2. What is your greatest challenge in giving earnest heed to the word of the kingdom? What is a strategy you can implement to help with this? Discuss this with your friend.

3. As a result of this chapter and our discussion I will:

4. I will start on:

---

[1] "Rugby Player Bitten by Lion He Tried to Stroke Reveals Horrifying Injuries," *The Independent*, 25 October 2017, http://www.independent.co.uk/sport/rugby/rugby-union/scott-baldwin-bitten-by-lion-south-africa-rugby-player-ospreys-injuries-hands-video-a8019081.html.

[2] "Rugby Player Bitten by Lion He Tried to Stroke Reveals Horrifying Injuries."

Chapter 4

He Restores the Kingdom

(2:5-18)

The author lives in Alabama. You may have seen or heard of us during football season. As of this writing, together, Auburn and Alabama account for 33 SEC titles, 25 by Alabama and 8 by Auburn. Both are among the winningest programs in college football history; Alabama is seventh while Auburn is sixteenth. The two share 22 national titles, Alabama with 17 and Auburn 5.[1]

"Auburn or Alabama?" is **the** question in our state. Seriously. Your footprints on your birth certificate are either blue and orange or crimson and white. As far as I know there has only been one wedding on game day (illegal procedure!) in my lifetime. Groomsmen gave smartphone updates during the ceremony, and multiple big screens made the reception beyond awesome.

Names like Joe Willie, Snake, Pat, Shug, Bear, Tubs, Cam or Bo all puff the chest. But despite tremendous athletes and crazy fan support, the long-term quality always goes back to the person behind the team—the coach. The better coach is the long-term advantage.

The Hebrews knew the Scriptures taught that angels were greater than humans, so how could the Son become man and be greater than them? He is clearly superior in several ways (1:5-14), but doesn't incarnation make Him inferior?

The answer is yes and no. Yes, He became **temporarily** lower than angels. No, because by incarnation He fulfilled a more excellent purpose than theirs.

He Restores Man's Destiny (2:5-9)

(5) [God] *did not subject to angels the world to come concerning which we are speaking. The world to come* was a common expression among Jews and Christians in the first century for Christ's kingdom, much as we say millennium. It reminds us that:

- There is a future kingdom coming on the earth.
- Kingdom life will resemble this life.
- Hebrews is about that kingdom.
- Angels will not rule that kingdom.

(6) God subjected the original earth to man (Gn 1:26-28). Our divinely designed destiny is to relate with Him and rule the earth under Him. David recorded His thoughts and feelings about this in Psalm 8:4-6, which the author quotes in verses 6-8:

> *What is man, that you remember him? Or the son of man, that you are concerned about him? You have made him for a little while lower than the angels; You have crowned him with glory and honor and have appointed him over the works of Your hands; You have put all things in subjection under his feet.*

(7) Throughout the Bible *son of man* refers to humanity or individuals (Nm 23:19; Ek 2:1) and suffering mankind (Mt 8:20; 17:22-23). Jesus' favorite self-designation was *Son of Man*, the promised God-Man-King who will rule forever (Dn 7:13-14; Mt 16:27-28). The author employs *man* and *son of man* in Psalm 8 to refer to both man in general and Jesus in particular.

We are temporarily beneath angels —*for you have made him for a little while lower than the angels*—until we rule them in the kingdom (1 Cr 6:2-3). As a greater man, the *Son* was also made lower than the angels for a brief time to rescue us from sin and restore our rule.

(8) David also noted that, *You have put all things in subjection under His* (Jesus' and our) *feet, but now we do not yet see all things subjected to him* (neither Jesus nor us). Why does Jesus not yet rule? He waits until the Father directs Him to return (1:13). Then He will subdue all enemies (Dn 7:23-27; Mt 13:41-43), redeem Israel (Dn 12:1-3; Zc 12:10-13:6; Rm 11:25-27) and reign.

We do not yet rule because Adam's sin corrupted our nature. It shattered the image of God and gave man's ruling authority to Satan (Lk 4:5-7). Our exalted role is derailed. We cannot ascend our throne and accomplish God's purpose. If man is going to rule the earth under God then someone else must recover our lost destiny for us.

(9) That someone is Jesus for *we do see Him who was made for a little while lower than the angels, namely, Jesus.* The author elevates the Son's humanity by calling Him *Jesus* for the first time. His incarnation qualified Him to reign over creation. How? *Because of the suffering of death* [Jesus is] *crowned with glory and honor.*

This is the first mention of a major theme in Hebrews—**suffering precedes and produces sovereignty**. From here on, the certainty that loyal endurance of suffering for following Jesus gains ruling glory runs through every chapter save one. We gain our thrones just as the High King did—by faithfully bearing trials (Lk 24:25-27; Mt 16:24-27; Lk 24:26; Ac 14:22; 2 Cr 4:16-18).

The Son's sufferings included death *so that by the grace of God He might taste death for everyone.* Grace was behind every pain, trial and the death that He endured. Grace sustained Him and saved us. Full and complete (*tasted*), Jesus' death sufficiently atoned for all men. However, what is potentially available to all is only actually realized in those who believe in Him. Those who believe in Jesus are born again and receive eternal life. Those who do not remain condemned (Jn 3:16-18).[2]

Through His incarnation, death and resurrection, Jesus has provided rescue from sin, regained the right to rule the earth as a man and received authority over all things (Mt 28:16-20). Believers share His spiritual authority now and may rule with Him later. That is the destiny for which God created us. Consider the possibilities placed before us! We are potential kings and queens—forever! Only Jesus could provide these privileges for angels cannot become incarnate.

He Brings Many Sons to Glory (2:10-13)

(10) *It was fitting* (right) for the Father to *perfect* Christ through sufferings. He did this to glorify believers: *in bringing many sons to glory*, that is, a fully restored state in the kingdom, conformed to Christ (Rm 8:18-21). Glory is never a place in the Bible; it is a state of being. Not all will share ruling glory, but all will be glorified and conformed to Christ.

The Father perfected His incarnate Son as the *author of their salvation* [from sin to inheritance] *through sufferings*. Jesus was never imperfect, but He had to be "fully formed" as the man to lead us back to the kingdom. Just as a clay pot is not wholly ready until it has been fired, so Jesus was not completely prepared to rule as a man until sufferings made Him so (Lk 24:36).

The Greek term *author* has several meanings, all of which would be appropriate here. He is the "prince" who leads to victory by suffering (Ac 3:15; 5:31). It may mean "pioneer" who blazes a new trail, or a "captain" who leads his troops through new territory. He is the "pathfinder" who cuts a new course across rough and unknown territory. He is the "champion" who fights single combat with the enemy on behalf of his people.

Whatever the proper translation, Jesus is the only one ready, willing and able to lead the way back to the kingdom. Fully perfected, He now experientially appreciates our struggles with sin and sufferings and uses them to prepare us for the kingdom. Only His incarnation allows for this.

(11) Jesus so identified Himself with humanity that He and believers became one kingdom family. He is our elder brother, *for both He who sanctifies* [positionally sets apart for the kingdom] *and those who are sanctified are all from one Father*. Jesus and the saints share both the same Father and destiny *for which reason He is not ashamed to call them brothers*. Being His siblings guarantees kingdom glory. Incredibly, regardless of our present progress or failure, He is never *ashamed* to recognize us as His brothers and sisters.

(12) The Father's plan and Jesus' work in bringing us to glory are so stunning that Jesus will celebrate it in millennial worship. The three-fold future tense *will* identifies these events as yet to come (vv. 12, 13).

Jesus will gather the family and preach about the Father: *I will proclaim Your name to My brethren,* then sing special music: *in the midst of the congregation I will sing Your praise.* The original context of the quote speaks of faithful endurance through desperate circumstances and refers to Jesus' reign after His sufferings on the tree (Ps 22:22).

I will put My trust in Him declares that persevering faith brought the Son and His family to the kingdom. Taken from Isaiah 18:17-18, its initial setting speaks of fidelity amid a disloyal generation prior to the Lord's return. So, Jesus will celebrate in the kingdom with those who arrived just as He did: enduring difficult times, even to death, by faith.

(13) Now the author uses Isaiah 8:18 to heighten the relationships between Jesus and His people: *behold, I and the children whom God has given Me.* Isaiah 53:10 indicates that the Suffering Servant *will see His offspring* [believers]. In some way in the kingdom we will be known as both Jesus' brothers and His children (Jn 11:32; 13:33; 21:5), a doubly intimate family relationship with the King.

Presently despised and discarded by family, friends and synagogue, Christ is using those challenges to ready the Hebrews for kingdom roles. There they will be feted as God's family, royal sons, brothers to the High King and even His children. He can do all this because He became man and bore great suffering, unlike the angels.

He Delivers from the Devil (2:14-16)

Jesus must *destroy the works of the devil* (1 Jn 3:8) to restore the kingdom. As the ideal man, He made provision to defeat and deliver from the devil, death and sin (17-18).

(14) *Therefore, since the children share in flesh and blood, He Himself likewise also partook of the same* to annul the devil's power

Jesus broke the rebel's power through an act of submission to God so *that through death He might render powerless him who had the power of death, that is, the devil.* The cross has not yet removed the devil's power of physical death but "put it in neutral" for saints as far as its effect.

We may die now, but Jesus will raise and remake our bodies, releasing them from the power of the grave (1 Th 4:13-18). In concluding the millennium, the Lord will vanquish both the leader of the rebellion and the last enemy. He will cast the devil into the lake of fire and brimstone forever, followed by both death and hades (Rv 20:10; 1 Cr 15:25-26, 54-58).

(15-16) Jesus also freed us from *slavery* to the *fear of death*. His resurrection and exaltation guarantee ours, so the fear of death is shackled. We may fear the process of death, but the black shadow itself has no substance.

This grace was for believers only *for assuredly, He does not give help to angels but He gives help to the descendant of Abraham.*

> Here "the seed of Abraham" probably refers primarily to believers, the spiritual descendants of Abraham (Gal. 3:29), rather than to Jews, the physical descendants of Abraham (cf. Isa. 41:8-10). The original readers, saved Jews, were both the physical and spiritual descendants of Abraham.[3]

Thanks to Jesus, physical death is only a sowing of seed that will result in a new immortal body ready for the kingdom.

He Frees from Sin (2:17-18)

(17) *He* [also] *had to be made like His brethren in all things so that He might become a merciful and faithful high priest in things pertaining to God.* Jesus the man knows in practice the demanding nature of a faithful walk along the narrow, steep, rocky trail to the kingdom. Having embraced the challenges and costs of discipleship, our high priest is *merciful* toward us and *faithful* to God.

We have a *high priest* in heaven who is just like us. He is a real man in heaven who feels our feelings and realizes our frailties.

As *high priest,* Jesus offered Himself rather than an animal *to make propitiation for the sins of the people.* The background of this verse is the Day of Atonement when Israel's high priest offered one annual sacrifice to cover God's righteous anger with the people for their sins. He also confessed the nation's sins over the scapegoat which was released into the wilderness to carry away the people's guilt for that year. But our high priest did not turn away wrath, sin and guilt annually; He put it away eternally by His death on the cross. Christ fully and perfectly bore God's eternal wrath (Rm 3:23-26; 1 Jn 1:8-2:2).

(18) Incarnation not only made Him the perfect sacrifice in death; it exposed Him to the temptations of life. *For since He Himself was tempted in that which He has suffered, He is able to come to the aid of those who are tempted.* Jesus was fully tempted to sin and truly tested by life's trials but came through them all spotlessly.

A mother who has gone through the trying birth process can best help a mother at her first delivery because she has experienced it. She grasps it. Because He knows the power of temptation, Jesus literally "runs close to help us" when tested, tempted and discouraged.

Sin broke our fellowship and squandered our rulership. But the Lord promised a specially born, male, warrior-rescuer to renew life and restore our rule (Gn 3:14-15). That promised one is Jesus the incarnate Son.

As a man, He restored our destiny as servant kings. He is the past provision for sin, our present high priest and future kingdom ruler, of which no angels are capable.

If we are to be counted among His companions, we will need the help of the great King-Priest-Son. The writer will explore the aid of Jesus' superior royal high priesthood and exhort us to avail ourselves of it in chapters 3:1-10:18.

Positioning for Companionship

1. Share your major take–away from this chapter with your brother or sister.

2. What do you think and feel about the opportunity to reign with Jesus? Stunned? Motivated? Confused? Unworthy? Humbled? Discuss this with your friend.

3. As a result of this chapter and our discussion I will:

4. I will start on:

[1] WIKIPEDIA, s.v. "Iron Bowl." (07 March, 2018). https://en.wikipedia.org/wiki/Iron_Bowl

[2] Bob Wilkin, "Is Forgiveness Available to All?" *FaithAlone.Org*, 28 March 2018, https://faithalone.org/magazine/y1988/88may3.html.

[3] Thomas L. Constable, "Notes on Hebrews" (2015): 35.

Section 2

Companions Draw Near the King–Priest–Son

(3:1-10:18)

God's desire for believers is priestly, royal companionship with His Son in His kingdom. That honor demands our perseverance as faithful royal–priests through tests and temptations, fears and struggles. This section focuses on Jesus' provision for His priest's endurance. It includes His high priestly character and call (3:1-5:10) and His order and covenant (7-8) that enables His eternally sufficient work (9:1-10:18). He provides everything that Judaism cannot so that we can endure to companionship.

Chapter 5

He Is a More Faithful High Priest

(3:1-6)

The author now expands the idea *merciful* and *faithful high priest* from 2:17 in reverse order. Chapter 3:1–6 describes Jesus' better faithfulness than Moses to lay the foundation for the second warning (3:7–4:13). He then depicts the Lord's better mercy than Aaron's priesthood (4:14–5:10).

Moses' name occurs 718 times in the Old Testament. He was Judaism's heart and soul, its founder, authority, icon and focal point. He liberated the people, led them through the Red Sea, carried the tablets of the Law and ratified the covenant. Moses built the tabernacle, ordained the priesthood and authored the Pentateuch. The entire Jewish worship system came from God through Moses. But Jesus is greater! How?

Jesus Has Better Offices (3:1)

(1) Believers are *holy brethren*, set apart as positional members of Jesus' royal family (2:11). We are also positional *partakers* [Gk. metochoi; companions] *of a heavenly calling* to be His kingdom partners (1:9, 14; 2:10; 3:14; 1 Pt 2:5-10; Rv 1:6). *Therefore,* [we must] *consider Jesus the Apostle and High Priest of our confession.*

In the culture, apostles were agents Rome deployed to found new cities or colonies. They came with the Emperor's authority as spokesmen, leaders and representatives

As our *Apostle*, Christ came to reveal the Father through His words and works (Jn 14:7-11) and to disclose Himself to the world as the Savior–King, the object of faith (Jn 11:27; 20:31). Jesus also brought grace and truth in His own person (Jn 1:17; Ti 2:11).

In contrast, God sent Moses to reveal His person and word to Israel and Pharaoh (Ex 3:13–22; 5:1-2) and to declare the law (Jn 1:17). So as revealer and leader, Jesus exceeds Moses.

Jesus is also the *High Priest of our confession*. Moses was a priest (Ps 99:6) but not a high priest and so could not offer an atoning sacrifice. In contrast, Jesus is our royal high priest. The Hebrews had publicly affirmed their belief in Jesus at their baptism. To return to Judaism would be to publicly renounce their *confession* of belief in Him.

Therefore, the author commands them to *consider* or "fix their minds" squarely on Jesus *the Apostle and High Priest of our confession*. We do what we think and go where we gaze.

Jesus Has Better Faithfulness (3:2)

(2) *He was faithful to Him who appointed Him, as Moses also was in all His house.* This is the first of seven uses of *house* in this paragraph. In verses 2-5, *house* is the tabernacle, Israel's place of worship. Verse 6 indicates the church, Christ's *house* of royal priests. We are His priestly *house* and serve Him as priests (1 Pt 2:5-10; 1 Tm 3:15; Rv 1:5–6; Hb 10:19–25; 12:28; 13:15-16). Our task is to faithfully function as His *house* or we can face temporal judgment and loss of reward.

Dependable might have been Moses' middle name. God Himself described Moses as trustworthy in all his roles in serving *in all His house* (Nm 12:7). Yet, in contrast, Jesus *was* [Gk. is being] *faithful to Him who appointed Him*. He is forever faithful whereas Moses was faithful.

Jesus Is a Better Person (3:3-6a)

(3-4) For He has been counted worthy of more glory than Moses, by just so much as the builder of the house has more honor than the house. Moses faithfully built a copy of the heavenly tabernacle. However, Jesus is God who built all things including Moses, for every house is built by someone, but the builder of all things is God.

(5) *Moses was faithful in all His house as a servant* preparing Israel's worship system *for a testimony of those things which were to be spoken later*. Like a model that represents the original, the tabernacle and its system pointed to the new covenant realities that Jesus produced and the kingdom which He will bring (8:1-13; 10:5-10; Jn 1:14).

(6a) Though Moses' servant faithfulness was beyond dispute, *Christ was faithful as a Son over His house*. *Was faithful* is the translator's insert. It should probably read, "is faithful" as per verse two. However, the emphasis here is that Christ is **God's Son over** His house while Moses was **God's servant in** His house.

This is the author's first use of *Christ*, emphasizing His anointing as prophet, priest and king. *Son* focuses on His coming rule as

David's seed who will have a royal house forever (2 Sm 7:11, 13, 16). Therefore, *house* in this verse refers to Jesus' household of king–priests, the church. We are the Son's royal priestly house by position (10:19–25; 1 Tm 3:15; 1 Pt 2:5-10; Rv 1:5–6).

However, we must remain faithful to Him and consistently practice our priestly roles to fully receive our kingdom inheritance (3:7-19; 10:19-39; 12:28; 13:15-19). We are His house *if* [Gk. maybe we will, maybe we won't] *we hold fast our confidence* [endure] *and the boast* [confession] *of our hope firm until the end*, that is death or the Rapture.

Since being His house is conditional on endurance, defectors to Judaism would forfeit their present privileges to worship Jesus, pray boldly, bear witness, encourage one another and serve the household. Withdrawing would open them to God's temporal judgment and cost them some or possibly all their kingdom roles. Consistent ministry to, with and among God's people, not just passive attendance at church services, remains a primary role for contemporary readers. We must be regularly involved in the ministry of believer priests.

Jesus is Better Than Moses	
Moses	**Jesus**
Priest (Ps 99:6)	Apostle and High Priest (1)
Sent from the desert (Ex 3)	Sent from heaven (1)
Was faithful to Him (2)	Is [Gk.] faithful to Him (2)
Part of the house (3)	The builder of the house (3)
A man who was built (4)	God who built all things (4)
Faithful in God's House (2, 5)	Faithful over God's House (5)
As a servant (6)	As a Son (5)
A testimony for later (5)	The fulfiller of the testimony (6)
Good	**Best**

Magnificent Moses was God's faithful old covenant servant, yet Jesus exceeds him far and away. Therefore, the Hebrews must not return to the Mosaic system. Rather, they must imitate Jesus' faithfulness to God and continue to serve as His priestly house.

Positioning for Companionship

1. Share your major take–away from this chapter with your brother or sister.

2. What is your greatest area of faithfulness as a praying, encouraging, witnessing, serving priest? How do you know? Weakest? Why? Discuss this with your friend.

3. As a result of this chapter and our discussion I will:

4. I will start on:

Chapter 6

Warning:
Be Faithful

(3:7-4:13)

About 610,000 people die of heart disease in the United States every year–that's 1 in every four deaths. It is the leading cause of death for both men and women. Heart disease, specifically hardening of the heart, is a profound spiritual disease among believers. And it can kill you.[1]

The first warning pointed out the danger of neglecting Christ's kingdom word and drifting away. In this one, the author explains the deadly threat of disbelief and disobedience because of a hard heart.

He builds his warning on several terms and concepts drawn primarily from Psalm 95:7-11 and Numbers 13-14 about Israel's refusal to enter the land. These include *voice, harden, hearts, rest, today* and *wrath*.

God had already given Israel title to the land and pledged that He would attend them as they conquered it (Dt 1:26-35). It was theirs to possess.

Before entry, He commanded Moses to send twelve spies to recon the land (Nm 13:1-20). Forty days later they returned and reported (Nm 13:25-14:10). Ten disbelievingly said, "No!", fearful of the challenges and enemies they had seen. Two said, "Go!" for they believed God

The land inheritance was Israel's reward for the taking by belief and obedience. Except for the two resolute stalwarts, God's people had made an irrevocable decision. They all ended up dead in the wilderness without inheritance except for Caleb and Joshua. God's love is everlasting, and His grace is free, but His patience has an expiration date.[2]

Long term pressures and persecution were affecting the reader's hearts. Some were on the verge of irreversible rebellion. Thus, connecting to 3:6, the author urges them to be a different people, a faithful house of priests, and embrace their opportunity to enter God's rest. To do so, they must guard their hearts.

The author makes his warning beginning in 3:7-19. He uses *if* and *therefore* to tie it directly to Christ's model of faithfulness in 3:1-6:

> *Christ was faithful as a Son over His house, whose house we are, if we hold fast our confidence and the boast of our hope firm until the end. Therefore, just as the Holy Spirit says, "Today if you hear His voice, do not harden your hearts as when they provoked Me, as in the day of trial in the wilderness..."* (3:6-7)

Guard Your Hearts (3:7-19)

Faithfulness comes from the heart, the place of thought, decisions and emotion. How do we guard it?

Hear God's Voice Today (3:7-11)

(7) *Today, if you hear His voice,* [Gk. perhaps you do, perhaps you don't] *do not harden your hearts as when they provoked Me, as in the day of trial in the wilderness. Today* designated the Israelites one life to accomplish their God given mission to inherit the land. But their disbelief and disobedience ran out the clock and they lost the game.

Sensing the same possibility among the Hebrews, the author repeated the word *Today* five times (3:7, 13, 15; 4:7 [twice]) to emphasize the fleeting occasion to prepare our quality of life in the kingdom. The Hebrews struggles could work for or against them in that regard depending on their response. The reality of *Today* calls for decisive action. We have only one Christian life and we don't know how long it will last. We must decide *Today* to live for the long tomorrow.

His voice refers to God's promises to take Israel into the land. In Hebrews, that voice is Jesus' better revelation.

(8-9) Israel *hardened* their hearts (3:8, 15; 4:7), went *astray,* and was willfully *ignorant of* God's *ways* (3:10). Their hearts were *evil* and *unbelieving* (3:12).

What made them like this? God said that *they did not know My ways.* He had shown His grace and power through Passover, Exodus, the Red Sea, water in the desert, and many others. However, they dwelt on their circumstances rather than on His capacity. That is the heart of the hard heart—a focus on situations rather than God's person, word and care.

(10-11) What was His response? *Therefore I was angry with this generation. . . as I swore in My wrath, "They shall not enter My rest."* They suffered God's temporal anger and lost everything. All believers whose inner man becomes calloused face the same danger. As Proverbs 4:23 says, *watch over your heart with all diligence, for from it flow the springs of life.*

Encourage One Another Daily (3:12-15)

(12-13) *Take care, brethren, that there not be in any one of you an evil, unbelieving heart that falls away from the living God.* Believers do develop *evil* hearts (Lk 11:13; 1 Cr 5:13; Jm 2:4). We can easily fail to believe God, especially when facing a big test, as did Israel (Nm 14:4, 9; Dt 1:6). Calloused hearts produce horrible catastrophes.

Note that the Holy Spirit used plural nouns, pronouns and verbs in the passage to spotlight the communal nature of the sin. As a priestly fellowship we share responsibility for one another's spiritual health (10:19-25). Since *any one of you* can fall away, we are to *encourage one another day after day, as long as it is still called "Today," so that none of you will be hardened by the deceitfulness of* [Gk. the] *sin.*

Any sin is deceptive in that it exaggerates the benefits of disobedience and diminishes the consequences. Thus, it hardens the heart and harms one in the long run.[3]

In contrast, authentic encouragement given and received protects from God's anger and promotes perseverance. God designed us to walk together. We need someone to challenge us, confront us, hug us and hear us regularly—*Today*. Moreover, they need the same from us. The healthy church community is a powerful protectant.

(14-15) The reason for mutual care is that *we have become partakers* [Gk. metochoi] *of Christ, if we hold fast* [Gk. maybe, maybe not] *the beginning of our assurance firm until the end while it is said, "Today if you hear His voice do not harden your hearts, as when they provoked Me."*

Assurance carries the idea of confidence that leads one to act. The author wants them to pursue companionship *until the end,* that is, death or the Rapture. It is the good finish that leads partnership.

There is one other protective practice.

Fear God's Wrath (3:16-19)

(16-17) *For who provoked Him when they had heard? Indeed, did not all those who came out of Egypt led by Moses? And with whom was He angry* *for forty years? Was it not with those who sinned, whose bodies fell in the wilderness?* The Israelites were a mostly regenerate nation. They had believed God's promise of rescue (Ex 3:13-18; 4:29-31) and He called them *My people* (Ex 5:1; Ps 95:6-7), yet still they felt is anger.

Many assume that God's wrath is only for the lost in eternity. In reality, both Testaments record God's **temporal** anger toward believers and unbelievers.

His earthly wrath is His active displeasure against sin. Sometimes He expresses it directly (Nm 16:21-35) and sometimes indirectly (Rm 13:1-5).

Complaining, greedy Israelite believers experienced it (Ex 14:31; Nm 11:1, 10, 33). He intended to kill Moses for failing to circumcise his son (Ex 4:24-26). Aaron and Miriam suffered His anger for speaking against Moses (Nm 12:9). Moses and Aaron both suffered God's wrath and forfeited their inheritance for striking the rock (Nm 20:6-13; 27:12-14; Dt 4:21-24).

In the New Testament, anyone who suppresses God's truth, believer or unbeliever, resides under His temporal wrath (Rm 1:18; 2:1). Any saint who continues in sin (Rm 5:9) or wrongfully disobeys government (13:1-5) faces it. A believer who hardens his or her heart or despises Christ and his inheritance will receive God's vengeance (Hb 10:26-31).

While God is very patient with His sinning people, there is a point of no return when His temporal wrath falls.

But how can God express His wrath against His own? Did not Christ's propitiation deal with that?

Many of God's works have a now-then quality. For instance, believers are already redeemed (Ep 1:7) yet our redemption still awaits (Ep 1:14; Rm 8:23). We are adopted as sons (Ep 1:5) but will be adopted in the future (Rm 8:23). We are spiritually resurrected in Christ (Rm 6:8–14), but our bodily resurrection is yet to occur (1 Cr 15:22, 52).

God's wrath operates similarly. His eternal wrath against all men was justly satisfied at the cross (Rm 3:25-26; 1 Jn 2:2). One escapes it by simple belief in Christ (Jn 5:24). All persons, believers or unbelievers, can escape His temporal wrath by repentance. Jonah 3-4 beautifully illustrates this.

(18-19) *And to whom did He swear that they would not enter His rest, but to those who were disobedient? So we see that they were not able to enter because of unbelief.* The term for *unbelief* is literally "disbelief."

Although God forgave, Israel's disbelief brought life under His anger for forty years (Nm 14:27–38). Yet, until the end of that period, God's covenant love remained unchanged. He freely and faithfully provided food, water, clothes, direction, protection, worship and forgiveness. Even so, the wasteland became their cemetery and their inheritance was forfeit.

This is the warning of 3:7-19: disbelief can produce disobedience that can result in death and disinheritance. Therefore, hear God's voice, encourage one another daily and fear God's wrath. Guard your heart.

Work Now to Enter Rest (4:1-13)

The author concludes the stern warning with encouragement. *Rest* remains available to all, but only the believing and diligent will obtain it.

We met the term *rest* in 3:11, 18, where God swore that the Exodus generation would not enter it. The author employs the idea nine more times in 4:1-11 with *rest, rested, Sabbath rest, His rest* or *My rest*. But what is *rest*?

Two things help us understand it. First is the Hebrews understanding of *rest* from the Old Testament (Dt 3:18-20; 12:8-10; 25:19; Js 1:13-17; 21:45, etc.). It was the inheritance of the land and the unending satisfaction of full life as a reward after they entered and conquered all the land. We might call it Canaan rest.

Thus, the Hebrews saw *rest* as a reward of the inheritance. It came after faithful obedience to the end of the assignment and could be lost by refusing to expend the effort needed to gain it.

The text itself gives us numerous traits of *rest* for church age believers. The author refers to as Companionship *rest*.

- It is God's rest. Of the 11 uses, 10 make God the source or model of it.
- It is a reward for works, not salvation by grace (3:12, 16; 4:1-3, 9-11)
- It is conditional on enduring faith and obedience (3:7-11-18; 4:10-11)
- It is timelessly available to every generation of believers (4:1, 6–11)
- It is entered after the completion of labors (4:2, 10)
- All believers will be in the kingdom but only some will inherit rest (4:6)
- It is received at the judgment seat (4:12-13)
- It is enjoyed in the kingdom (Ps 132:12-14; Is 11:10; 14:3; 32:18).

is a millennial reward offered only to church age believers. Like Canaan rest it requires that we complete our task until the end. It appears to be abundant life in the kingdom that enjoys a unique camaraderie with the King, including depth of relationship and kingdom functions. Companions will be a cadre of unique friends and co-laborers. We will *rest* in full reward.

The writer will repeat his main points over and again: *rest* is available, it can be lost or gained based on one's heart response and works, and we need each other to do so. What tasks are necessary to obtain it?

Believe the Good News of Rest (4:1-5)

(1) In light of the clear and present danger of missing *rest* the author reiterates the emphasis on mutual priestly care. If the old covenant saints failed to enter it, then new covenant saints can too. *Therefore, let us fear if, while a promise remains of entering His rest, any one of you may seem to have come short of it.* None of the Hebrews has yet succumbed to the danger of disbelief, but it doesn't mean that it won't happen, so they must guard each other. The promise remains and believers must work together to ensure that all realize it.

(2) *For indeed we have had good news preached to us, just as they also; but the word they heard did not profit them, because it was not united by faith in those who heard.* What good news did both groups hear? It was not the gospel of how to be born again. Israel was a saved people (Ex 4:29-31; Ps 95:6-7) as were the Hebrews. Instead, they refused to believe God's gracious promise of inheriting a land of milk and honey and rejected the works necessary to receive it (Ex 3:15-17; 6:2-9; 13, 11; Nm 10:29; 13:30; Dt 1:7-8, 26-35).

(3) The Hebrews (and us) must make faith profitable and act on the promises. *We who have believed enter* [Gk. are entering] *that rest* emphasizes that future rest demands a steadfast belief in the present. The Greek verb *enter* is present tense. Some understand it to mean that we are enjoying spiritual rest now (Mt 11:28-30), which is possible but doesn't fit the context well. Others see it as a futuristic present, meaning that it refers to the kingdom, which is also possible. Better, it seems that the tense indicates we are currently preparing for future rest by our present day to day responses to God.

Just as He has said, As I swore in My wrath, "They shall not enter My rest," although His works were finished from the foundation of the world. God offered *rest* from the beginning but those who refuse to work for it lose it.

(4-5) *For He has said somewhere concerning the seventh day: "And God rested on the seventh day from all His works."* The writer uses God's *seventh day* rest to illustrate that it follows completed work.

The Creator was certainly not tired; rather on the first rest day He enjoyed total pleasure and delight in the quality of His **finished** work. We must complete our works now to enjoy our "very good" as God did, for *again in this passage, "They* [who do not finish faithfully] *shall not enter My rest."*

Obey to Enter That Rest (4:6-9)

(6) *It remains for **some** [believers] to enter it.* Again, all believers will be in the kingdom but just as our roles will differ, so will the possession of rest.

Those who formerly had good news preached to them [the Exodus generation] *failed to enter because of disobedience,* even Aaron and Moses (Dt 32:48-52; 34:1-5).

(7-8) Still, God graciously offers *rest* to every generation. *He again fixes a certain day, "Today," saying through David after so long a time just as has been said before, "TODAY IF YOU HEAR HIS VOICE, DO NOT HARDEN YOUR HEARTS."* The promise remained in Joshua's day, David's day, the Hebrews day and continues today, *for if Joshua had given them rest, He would not have spoken of another day after that.*

Be Diligent to Enter That Rest (4:10-11)

(9-10) *So there remains a Sabbath rest for the people of God. For the one who has entered His rest has himself also rested from his works, as God did from His.*

> The idea of Sabbath rest was a phrase for the kingdom in Judaism. "A traditional Shabbat prayer with a lengthy heritage is, "May the All Merciful let us inherit the day which shall be wholly a Sabbath and rest in the life everlasting."[4]

(11) *Therefore let us be diligent to enter that rest, so that no one will fall, through following the same example of disobedience.* To be *diligent* is to obediently fulfill our mission together as His priestly house (3:6-7, 8, 12-13, 4:1-2). We must faithfully obey His commands and endure suffering for His sake if called upon, both individually and as a member of the priestly house.

Believers who neglect or forsake the community are in danger of mimicking Israel and falling as did those *whose bodies fell* [note the wordplay of *fall* with *fell*] *in the wilderness* (3:17). No one is immune so *let us be diligent* to watch ourselves and one another.

Finally, we must envision our future appraisal to enter *rest*.

Prepare for Evaluation Before Rest (4:12-13)

(12) The author has repeatedly warned and encouraged the brothers with Psalm 95, Numbers 14, Joshua, Genesis 2 and his letter. Now he reminds them that God's word will be the instrument with which Christ will judge their hearts at the Judgment Seat. *For the word of God is living and active and sharper than any two-edged sword*. Scripture slices to the core of our being, *piercing as far as the division of soul and spirit, of both joints and marrow*. That same voice we are to hear (3:7) *is able to judge the thoughts and intentions of the heart* that we are not to harden (3:8).

(13) *And there is no creature hidden from His sight, but all things are open and laid bare to the eyes of Him with whom we have to do.* As we explain ourselves to Him, we will be unsheltered as the throat of a sacrificial animal was exposed before the knife of the priest. His *eyes* will examine every one of our works that sharply, so we should fear this and act accordingly. See Appendix 4.

The Exodus generation lost their lives and their inheritance through disbelief and disobedience. Recalling this, the writer alerted the Hebrews to guard their hearts or they could lose their lives and companion rest.

To obtain companionship, we must believe the promise of it, obey the Lord and work diligently to fulfill our mission and finish well. This is not just an individual responsibility – we are o run together with other saints and help one another. The decisions we make to press on or to retreat will gain us much or cost us much in the kingdom. Let us labor *Today* to rest tomorrow.

Positioning for Partnership

1. Share your major take-away from this chapter with your partner.

2. What is one area in which you struggle to be consistently obedient or faithful? Why do you think this is so? How can another believer help you improve?

3. As a result of this chapter and our discussion I will:

4. I will start on:

---

[1] "Heart Disease Facts & Statistics | Cdc.Gov," 28 November 2017, https://www.cdc.gov/heartdisease/facts.htm.

[2] Charles R., Swindoll, *Abraham: One Nomad's Amazing Journey of Faith*, Kindle. (Tyndale House Publishers, Inc., 2014), 1637.

[3] Thomas D. Lea, *Hebrews & James*, vol. 10 of *Holman New Testament Commentary* (Broadman & Holman Publishers, 1999), 50.

[4] Steven Ger, *The Book of Hebrews: Christ Is Greater* (Chattanooga, TN: AMG Publishers, 2009), 85.

Chapter 7

He Is a Great High Priest
(4:14-5:10)

Want some fun? Ask any two golfers over 25 who is the greatest: Jack Nicklaus or Tiger Woods? Like junkyard dogs they will immediately bark "Nicklaus" or "Tiger" and chew on each over contrasting wins, equipment, quality of competition, playing through injuries, etc.

Based on their slide back to temple worship, some of the Hebrews needed to realize there was no debate over how superior Jesus' high priesthood was to Aaron's. Chapter 2:17 described Jesus as a *merciful* and *faithful* high priest. Having revealed and applied His faithfulness in 3:1-4:13, now the author focuses on Jesus' better high priestly mercy and ministry.

He Has a Superior Position (4:14a, 16a)
(14a) *Therefore* ties us back to 4:1-13. To help us attain millennial rest *we have* [Gk. are having] *a great high priest*. Jesus' exalted position is thrice superior to Aaron's. Unlike Aaronic priests, He never sleeps, leaves or gets too busy to hear and help us.

He has also *passed through the heavens* whereas the Aaronic high priest could only pass through the earthly veil (Lv 16:2). Scripture presents three heavens, the atmosphere, space and God's dwelling (1 Kg 8:22, 27; 2 Cr 12:2) which makes Christ's passage far better.

(16a) Finally, our great high priest sits on *the throne of grace* beside the Father. Aaron and his descendants could only briefly stand in God's presence once a year in the earthly tabernacle. But Jesus is matchless. He is ever-present, exalted and enthroned.

He Is a Superior Person (4:14b)

(14b) *Jesus the Son of God* perfectly unites deity and humanity. Jesus the man experienced our feelings, temptations, pain, grief, disappointments and love.

He knows what it's like to be the oldest child in a house full of siblings. From youth, He worked hard and interacted with differing difficulties, deadlines and customers. As a teen, His parents misunderstood Him. In His adult years, Jesus grappled with incredible demands on His time, shattered sleep, gross misunderstandings, interrupted conversations, deep, deep weariness and betrayal by friends. But He also had fun at a wedding, loved dinner parties, embraced friends across the social spectrum and was deeply moved by the hopeless and helpless. He fully fathoms our life.

But many priests may have the same experiences. Why is Jesus better? He is *the Son of God*, so God has a human heart. He empathizes with all of us and can aid each of us. Jesus is indeed greater, so *let us hold fast our confession* regardless of opposition.

He Makes Superior Provision (4:15-16)

(15) *We do not have a high priest who cannot sympathize with our weaknesses.* Because He is a man, Jesus knows how difficult faithfulness is and how fragile we are when tempted and tested. Imperfect men, including high priests (and modern spiritual leaders), can misjudge or vilify weaknesses as did Eli with Hannah (1 Sm 1:13). They can be consumed with position and power as were Annas and Caiaphas (Mt 26:3, 54-67). But not Jesus.

Having been where we are, He is *One who has been tempted in all things as we are* (Mt 16:23; Lk 4:13). But Jesus successfully passed every test of human nature *without sin*. Our struggles with tests easily turn into temptation, and the temptation often becomes a sin. Jesus never failed a test or yielded to temptation by omission or commission. He is better qualified to assist us through the struggles of discipleship than any other priest could ever be. See Appendix 5.

(16) No eastern king allowed free access to his presence. Anyone who approached unbidden could earn an instant death penalty (Es 5:1-2). Those invited to stand before the king did so in postures of humility, with very cautious speech and happy faces, for no one could be sad or speak wrongly in the king's presence (Nh 2:1-2).

But Jesus, enthroned in heaven, bids us, flawed and weak, *draw near with confidence* or "open speaking." We need not beg Him or denigrate ourselves. We can tell Him all our fears and flaws, report the sin that appeals, express our confusion, and ask our questions. We can cry out to Him with no pretense and no feeling of "I can't bother Him with this." Having walked a lifetime in our sandals, He is delighted when we *draw near* to Him with confident honesty.

When we are weak, we need strength, and when we stumble, we need compassion and help to get back up or stand firm. Whenever we confidently draw near, Jesus discharges *mercy* and *grace* like Niagara Falls pours water.

Mercy is Jesus' felt response to our misery. It is His compassion in action that reduces, removes, or relieves distress (Mt 14:14; Mk 1:41; Lk 7:13-14). We also will *find grace* at His throne.

There are many types of grace such as saving grace (Ep 2:9-10), giving grace (2 Cr 8:1-9), ruling grace (Rm 6:14) and God's enabling grace (2 Cr 12:7-10). At *the throne of grace,* we will *find grace to help* [Gk. hold together] *in time of need* [Gk. at the right time]. Helping grace doesn't come early, but only when we are in the crucial situation.

Acts 27:16-17 describes Paul's transport ship to Rome breaking apart in a furious storm. Imagine the planks screeching and separating as frigid water blows over the gunwale, sweeps the decks and spews into the bilge. Sails slap like thunder. Waves sledgehammer the sides, and irresistible wind shrieks through the ropes.

As a last resort, the crew desperately wraps the ship with rope and cranks it tight, *undergirding* it (27:17), thus holding it together just in time. This *undergirding* is the term *help* in Hebrews 4:16. Jesus winches us together just when we are at the point of breaking up. That is helping grace!

Jesus is our great high priest. His *merciful* heart responds to our misery and His *gracious* hands enable us to endure. Therefore, *let us draw near* to Him for help to *hold fast our confession.*

He Has a Superior Placement (5:1-10)

Jesus also has more exclusive placement into the priesthood than the Aaronic high priests. This paragraph contrasts His qualifications and ordination with Aaron and his descendants.

Aaronic Placement (5:1-6)

(1a) He must be a man from the right order. One qualification was that *every high priest taken from among men* must be a direct male descendant of Aaron (Ex 28:1; Nm 18:7). In this way, the high priest would be separate from the rest of the people, yet at the same time, part of the nation from the tribe of Levi. He shared identity with those whom he served.

(1b, 3) He must offer repeated sacrifices. Through the centuries, Jewish priests and high priests offered countless daily and annual sacrifices to cover the guilt of sins. The high priest offered for himself first on the yearly Day of Atonement, for he was as needy as the rest of Israel. *Every high priest is appointed on behalf of men in things pertaining to God, in order to offer both gifts and sacrifices for sins . . . and because of it he is obligated to offer sacrifices for sins, as for the people, so also for himself.*

(2) He must be sympathetic with sinful men. Though not required in the Law, sympathy is a desired trait for a priest, for then *he can deal gently with the ignorant and misguided, since he himself also is beset with weakness.* Hopefully his frailties made a high priest tender, kindhearted and patient with others.

(4) He must be called by God. Aaron's appointment to the priesthood was God's gracious gift to him and his family. *And no one takes the honor to himself but receives it when he is called by God, even as Aaron was.* The priesthood was God's idea, and He determined who would be the priests.

To attempt to appoint oneself was sheer folly and self–destruction. Korah and his family lost their lives (Nm 16). Saul forfeited his kingdom (1 Sm 13:8-14) and King Uzziah lost his health and capacity to rule, being made physically and spiritually unclean (2 Ch 26:16-21). Unassuming reception of the priestly office rather than independent self-assertion is the emphasis.

Jesus' Placement (5:5-10)

How does Jesus compare? The author highlights His superior qualifications in reverse order to those of Aaron.

(5) Jesus has a better call. Like Aaron, *Christ did not glorify Himself so as to become a high priest.* Even though God previously anointed Him as *Christ* [prophet, priest and king], Jesus meekly waited on God's appointment to the priesthood. His selection is twice better. First, God spoke directly to Him: *He who said to Him.* God gave directions **about** Aaron's ordination whereas He made a declaration **to** Jesus. Second, God also declared Him to be King,

"You are My Son, Today I have begotten You," (1:5; Ps 2:7) and so He is called as Priest-King, not just priest.

(6) Aaron and every descendant high priest died. In stunning contrast, the Father declared to Jesus, *"You are a priest forever according to the order of Melchizedek."* The author will tell us more about Melchizedek shortly.

(7) Jesus has better sympathy. Jesus suffered much *in the days of His flesh,* and the most difficult may have been in Gethsemane when *He offered up both prayers and supplications with loud crying and tears.* We know the physical prospect of the cross and its attending flogging was genuinely terrifying, but Jesus did not seek release from it (Mk 10:45; Jn 10:17-18; Ac 4:27-28; Gl 1:4; 2:20; Ph 2:8; Hb 10:5-10).

When Jesus *cried out to the One able to save Him from death,* He requested **endurance through** the passion rather than **exemption from** it. He literally asked for deliverance "out of" death, not from it. *He was heard because of His piety*—His total abandonment to His Father's will, regardless of cost.

God indeed delivered Jesus out of death, but only after His sufferings. The resurrection and exaltation completely reversed all that occurred in the betrayal, the Garden, the trials, on Golgotha and in the tomb. Now He sits, awaiting the full inauguration of His kingdom.

Like Jesus, the Hebrews may continue to suffer in God's will, but the result of their perseverance will be eternal glory and joy after they go through the pain (1:9; 12:2).

(8) *Although He was a Son, He learned obedience from the things which He suffered.* "This is the sole New Testament verse in which Jesus is the subject of the verb learn."[1] The King did not need to learn how to obey but rather to experience the cost of obedience in a disobedient world. A lifetime of trials gave Him firsthand awareness of all that human submission to God entails. Indeed, He learned the cost of obedience unto death. The Hebrews may need His empathetic grace to do likewise (12:3-4).

(9) Jesus offered a better sacrifice. All of Christ's suffering, obedience, trials and tests led to the cross. His passion agonies were merely the last in a lifelong process of *having been made perfect* (fully formed and functional).

Jesus is undoubtedly the source of eternal life, but that was not the author's meaning when he wrote *He became to all those who obey Him the source of eternal salvation*. Scripture is clear that one receives eternal life (Jn 3:16), God's righteousness (Rm 3:22) and forgiveness (Ep 1:7) by grace alone through faith alone in Jesus alone (Ep 2:8-9), not by obedience.

Obedience ought to follow faith for eternal life, but it is not required for it and may or may not do so. Nor, as we have seen, is obedient behavior the proof of belief.

All believers *who obey Him* despite their circumstances will receive *eternal salvation* or deliverance from the trials of life into kingdom inheritance.

(10) Jesus is of a better order. He was *designated by God as a high priest according to the order of Melchizedek,* a King–Priest as found in Genesis 14:17-20. Jesus' priesthood is more fully developed in chapter 7. The point of this repeated reference to *Melchizedek* is that Jesus' order is eternal and so superior.

God's promises of kingdom rest to those who persevere do not lessen the challenges of fidelity. Like the Hebrews, we struggle and stumble on our way. But Jesus is our great high priesthood. Draw near to Him.

To further highlight Jesus' preeminence, the author will explain more about the order of Melchizedek, but first he must challenge his readers to grow.

Positioning for Partnership

1. Share your major take–away from this chapter with your partner.

2. Recall a time or two when you experienced the helping grace of God in answer to prayer. How did it hold you together?

3. As a result of this chapter and our discussion I will:

4. I will start on:

---

[1] Thomas D. Lea, *Hebrews & James*, vol. 10 of Holman New Testament Commentary (Broadman & Holman Publishers, 1999), 93.

Chapter 8

Warning:

Press on to Maturity

(5:11-6:20)

You'd turn around and there he was. Very, very up close and personal. Staring at you through big, thick glasses. And you'd never hear him come in.

His speech was more grunts than words and when misunderstood he sometimes became quite agitated, which you didn't want.

About 6'1", he was thin, fast, long armed and Hercules strong. And so strong-willed.

The apartment complex had a 24' x 24' asphalt basketball court where he loved to play. He didn't jump and rarely moved from wherever he decided to stand. But when he shot it was a rainstorm of Benjamin's. The ball thundered off the square on the metal backboard and lightning—popped the net. Seemingly always.

Everybody wanted him on their team and because he was Stevie, no one dared try and block his shots.

Stevie was 16, a mentally disabled young man, around the age of three or four intellectually and emotionally, trapped in a growing body. He was snared in immature dysfunction for the rest of his life. He couldn't progress to full maturity.[1]

The prior warnings were against neglectful drifting from the word and willful disbelief of God's promised rest. Now the writer warns against deliberate regression from spiritual growth. It can end in the tragedy of unchanging immaturity and spiritual dysfunction that results in temporal punishment and lost inheritance.

The author picks up his previous mentions of Melchizedek, an enigmatic figure from Genesis 14 who was both king and priest. *Concerning him we have much to say*, he wrote. However, it was *hard to explain*. Why? Not because of the writer or the subject, but because of the readers: *since you have become dull of hearing*. In effect, the author is saying, "It is difficult to explain the high priestly work of Christ because you have become spiritually lethargic."

He rebukes (5:11-14), warns (6:1-8) and encourages them (6:9-20) so they will grow again, endure by faith and share in Christ's reign.

A Rebuke of Willful Immaturity (5:11-14)
The pointed reproach describes their intentional infancy. What does deliberate immaturity look like?

Laziness toward the Word (11)
(11) It's not that the Hebrews couldn't hear about Melchizedek—some of them wouldn't: *you have become dull* [Gk. lethargic or sluggish] *of hearing*.

Whereas once they had heard and applied the word, some had deliberately closed their hearts to it. It was dangerous to follow the message about Christ so they had stopped. They were no longer interested in hearing or living it.

Inability to communicate the Word (12a)
(12a) *By this time you ought to be teachers.* Over time, one mark of growth is the capacity to clarify what and why one believes. This doesn't mean that all must preach, teach a class, etc., but simply be able to spell out the basics of what he or she believes. Some could no longer do so. The old adage is true: if you don't use it you lose it, especially in the spiritual realm.

Needing an infant diet of the Word (12b)
(12b) In fact, *you have need again for someone to teach you the elementary principles of the oracles of God and you have come to need milk and not solid food.* Both spiritual milk and solid food are essential to growth. Even adults continue to need milk. Why then is a renewed need for the ABCs bad? Because they had *need again* and *had come* to need. Their spiritual diet and lifestyle had regressed.[2] What physically or spiritually healthy person regresses?

Immature babies cannot eat solid food nor act with maturity. In this context *milk* represents the ability to grasp and apply foundational truth (6:1-2; 1 Pt 2:1-3). *Solid food* is comprehending and practicing the word of the kingdom and the ministry of our Priest–King.

Lack of skill in applying the Word (13-14)
(13) The main point here about spiritual advance is that Biblical information is necessary but it is living what we know that produces growth. Spiritual babes do not live what they learn, *for everyone who partakes only of milk is not accustomed to* [Gk. inexperienced in] *the word of righteousness, for he is an infant.* The Hebrews were not babes in understanding—the previous chapters overflow with challenging truths. Their primary failure was implementation.

The Jewish philosophy of learning was that one knows something once he can apply it, which comes primarily from watching, hearing and doing. (Remember how Jesus trained the Twelve?) Our Western concept is grab the facts, regurgitate them and often forget them. Our learning is "I can tell." Theirs was "I can do." Some Hebrews were losing both capacities.

(14) The writer illustrates with the word–picture of working out at the gym. *But solid food is for the mature who because of practice* [application] *have their senses* [Gk. perceptions] *trained* [Gk. exercised] *to discern good and evil.* James, another Jewish believer made the same point with a different word picture: *prove yourselves doers of the word, and not merely hearers* [Gk. auditors] *who delude themselves.*

The terms *senses, good* and *evil* include righteous ethics and morals (13:1-6) but primarily speak to decision making with values and choices aligned with the Bible and the kingdom (11:1-12:3).

Spiritual progression requires comprehension plus application. Otherwise, there is digression that may end with judgment.

Caution About Severe Judgment (6:1-8)

Now the author warns his readers how dangerous deliberate dullness is.

God Must Permit Renewed Growth (1-3)

(1-2) *Let us press on to maturity.* He includes himself because no one has arrived and anyone can fall away. *Maturity* here includes the regular application of God's word (5:14), consistent service to the saints (6:9-10) and diligent endurance as we await rewards (6:11-20).

They needed to move on, *not laying again a foundation of repentance from dead works and of faith toward God, of instruction about washings and laying on of hands, and the resurrection of the dead and eternal judgment.* These three pairs summarize some foundational Christian teachings that gave fresh meanings to Jewish doctrines. This list is quite telling. It deals with salvation, the church and future things.

- *Repentance and faith*: rejecting the Levitical system and law–keeping for simple faith in Christ and a lifestyle of changed behavior–salvation.
- *Washings and laying on of hands*: the means of daily spiritual cleansing and training, recognizing and sending local and global ministry leaders–church.
- *Resurrection and judgment*: additional resurrections and judgments such as the Rapture, the Judgment Seat and the Great White Throne–future things.

New believer basics in the early church far exceeded what many experienced believers receive in churches today, and it all had direct application to daily life. And this was the baby's menu!

(3) A return to spiritual progress is not automatic. *Press on* is a passive verb meaning "let us be carried on" [by God's Spirit]. *This we will do, if God permits* [Gk. maybe He will, maybe He won't]. Though it would be only in very severe cases, it is possible to regress to the point where one cannot renew.

Once we deliberately step away, only God determines if we can grow again. He may choose to leave us in infancy!

God May Judge Rather than Restore (4-8)

The writer moves from *we, you,* and *us* to *those, them,* and *they* to avoid explicitly identifying the people described. He believes that they can still diligently advance and avoid the picture he's about to paint.

The warning clearly addresses believers for only saints need to mature. Unbelievers need to believe in Jesus for eternal life. It is also real; a hypothetical warning is not a warning. Finally, it is not about receiving or losing eternal life; it is about repentance of believers.

(4-5) The explanation for God's judgment. *Those who have once been enlightened* are those who were instructed in and believed the gospel (10:32). *Tasted of the heavenly gift* describes those who received eternal life, for *taste* is complete appropriation, the same term that describes Jesus tasting death in 2:9.

They *have been made partakers* [Gk. metochoi] *of the Holy Spirit* or indwelt by Him. As well, they had *tasted the good word of God and the powers of the age to come* by receiving the word about Christ and the kingdom and experiencing or witnessing a kingdom preview through apostolic miracles (2:3–4). Even with all this, some of the Hebrews chose willful lethargy. What a sad, dangerous and short-sighted decision!

(6) For those who *then have fallen away* by abandoning spiritual growth and Jesus for Judaism, *it is impossible to renew them again to repentance.*

Fallen away is the ongoing departure of drifting from the kingdom message, and so failing to trust God amid the challenges and press on to inheritance. Genuine believers can and do fall away from the faith (Gn 25:29-34; Nm 14:27-32; 1 Tm 4:1; 2 Tm 2:17-18; 4:3-4), but many more return.

However, some do not. Why is that? *It is impossible* [for God] *to renew* that person *to repentance* or growth (not eternal life or forgiveness) because He has chosen not to (2 Tm 2:24-26). This is why we cannot talk an indifferent, resistant believer into repentance. We are to still make every effort to restore him or her (Jm 5:19-20; Jd 1:22-23) for we don't know if he or she has crossed the line, and as priests we care for one another. But only God can bring a believer to repentance, which begins with His permission (2 Tm 2:24-25). Believer's repentance is a change of mind that yields changed behavior (2 Cr 7:8-11).

This does not include all believers who fall away from growth for we all know those who have returned. But, should God not permit repentance the defector will remain spiritually immature and ineffective. He will sacrifice any rewards he might have gained after that point. Dullness is a lose now, lose then choice.

Why might God deny repentance? *Because they again crucify to themselves the Son of God and put Him to open shame.* In a sense, they repeat the malice, disbelief, public rejection and repudiation, judgment and dishonor of those who crucified Christ (Mt 26:1-5; 27:1-2, 24-26; Mk 15:8-15; Lk 23:18-25; Jn 19:15). What an affront to the heart of God and the Savior–King.

(7) The illustration of judgment. *Ground that drinks the rain which often falls on it* represents believers who absorb and apply the rain of God's word. Such ground *brings forth vegetation useful to those for whose sake it is also tilled.* Growing saints are *useful* in God's hands to both the lost and the saved. They also receive *a blessing from God*, including further growth and progress toward rewards.

(8) *But if it yields thorns and thistles* [regression or denouncing Christ], *it is worthless* [Gk. disapproved]. This term refers to lost reward at the judgment seat (1 Cr 9:27) and includes the judgment described here. Such ground is *close to being cursed*. It does not say that God curses the ground nor that He does so every time—such believers are *close to being cursed.*

God cursed the ground in Genesis 3 and it bore thorns and thistles. He cursed Israel's ground with fruitlessness for forsaking Him (Dt 18:18, 20) and in judgment burnt the earth with its yield (Dt 32:22). The ground lost its ability to fully function as designed and to bless others just as regressing saints may do.

And it ends up being burned does not mean hell, for the ground remains; only the foliage is burnt even as farmers, ranchers and foresters do today. As stated above, burning is God's temporal judgment of a believer (Gn 19:24-25; Is 9:18-19; 10:17). In Hebrews it likely refers to experiencing uselessness, the coming destruction of Jerusalem or to other severe chastening such as death (1 Cr 11:30; 1 Jn 5:16). Whatever it is, it will undoubtedly diminish one's kingdom life for it will include loss of reward.

Encouragement to Endure (6:9-20)

(9) The author has been forthright, even severe, but he softens the blow here. He does not believe that any of his *beloved* ones are at the point of cursing for *we are convinced of better things concerning you and things that accompany salvation* [inheritance], *though we are speaking in this way*. Instead, he gives three stimuli to faith, patience and inheritance.

God Is Just to Reward (10-12)

(10) God will reward their past, present and future fidelity, for *God is not unjust so as to forget your work and the love which you have shown toward His name, in having ministered and in still ministering to the saints*. We express love for God when we serve one another (Jn 13:13-15, 34-35; 14:15) and He reciprocates with eternal reward.

(11-12) Since God will reward, *we desire that each one of you show the same diligence* in service, which is application of truth toward others. With such persistence, t*hey will realize the full assurance of hope until the end* and live with the confidence of companionship until death or the Rapture. The author wants that hope to open their ears *so that you will not be sluggish,* the same Greek term translated *dull of hearing* in 5:11. Rather than dullness, he desires their spiritual vitality as *imitators of those who through faith and patience* [applied truth] *inherit the promises.*

God Is Faithful to His Promises (13-18a)

Abraham is the prime model of one who inherited the promises *through faith and patience*. His test in the sacrifice of Isaac illustrates God's faithfulness to reward those who steadfastly endure trials (Gn 22).

When Abraham offered Isaac, for whom he waited 25 years, he still trusted God's earlier promises to multiply His offspring through Isaac even if the Lord had to raise him from the dead (11:17-19). This is what the Hebrews must do—continue to patiently trust and obey even though it appears loss and death may follow.

(13-15) After Abraham passed the test, God gave him a double guarantee that He would indeed deliver all that He had promised. *For when God made the promise to Abraham, since He could swear by no one greater, He swore by Himself, saying, "I WILL SURELY BLESS YOU AND I WILL SURELY MULTIPLY YOU."* The double warrant was God's *promise* and His oath. *And so, having patiently waited, he obtained the promise.* Abraham qualified to receive all that God could give because he endured by faith. So would the Hebrews. And so will we.

We sometimes appeal to a higher authority to end a disagreement, such as "So help me God," *for men swear by one greater than themselves, and with them, an oath given as* [Gk. legal] *confirmation is an end of every dispute.*[3] God swore on Himself by Himself and ended any further discussion with His legal affirmation. His promises are as true as He is for those endure.

(17-18a) Marvelously, *in the same way God, desiring even more to show to the heirs of the promise the unchangeableness of His purpose,* [to gather a company of companions for His Son] *interposed with an oath, so that by two unchangeable things in which it is impossible for God to lie.* His declaration is certain because He cannot lie (Nm 23:19; 1 Sm 15:29; Ti 1:2). There should be no doubt. God has both promised and sworn to reward endurance. His character guarantees His word.

Christ Has an Eternal Priesthood (18b-20)

(18b) Since God keeps His promises the author is concerned that *we who have taken refuge would have* [Gk. draw, as in 4:16] *strong encouragement to take hold* [Gk. hold fast or endure, cf. 4:14] *of the hope* [of reward] *set before us.*

Refuge reminds the readers of the six Levitical cities of refuge that were safe havens for those guilty of unintentional manslaughter. The person would live there securely until the death of the high priest who was in office at the time of the trial. If the attacker left the city of refuge before the death of the high priest, however, the avenger would have the right to kill him.[4]

The Hebrews had a better refuge. They were spiritual fugitives sheltering in Jesus, the eternal high priest who secures our hope of reward. He will never die and they need never fear. But if they left, they may again be culpable.

(19) *This hope we have as an anchor of the soul* [Gk. life].

> "Soul" (psuchē) may be the way to understand it, but the term is often used of the life of man and this seems to be the meaning here. The author is not simply saying that hope secures the "spiritual" aspect of man. He is affirming that hope forms an anchor for the whole of life. The person with a living hope has a steadying anchor in all that he does.[5]

(20) *This hope* of growth, glorification, inheritance, reward and companionship *is both sure and steadfast* because it is *one which enters within the veil* of the heavenly tabernacle *where Jesus has entered as a forerunner for us.*

In the ancient Mediterranean numerous harbors had breakwaters with narrow entrances. A forerunner was a small boat tethered to a larger ship outside the harbor. The sailors in the small craft would carry the ship's anchor within the harbor and secure it so the ship would not drift away (Ac 27:29-30). Jesus our high priest has made our hope of inheritance as secure as His presence in heaven. *Having become a high priest according to the order of Melchizedek,* He ever provides help to finish well.

Some Hebrew brothers had stopped practicing their faith to return to Judaism. Such public repudiation of Christ would result in a temporal judgment and eternal loss.

Instead, they must hear and apply God's word and patiently abide their circumstances. God's character and Jesus priesthood guarantees reward to those who continue to trust, obey and wait. This glorious provision brings the discussion full circle, back to Christ's Melchizedekian priesthood.

Positioning for Companionship

1. Share your major take–away from this chapter with your friend.

2. Application of Scripture is key to spiritual health and reward. Discuss with your companion how well you put "hands and feet" to what you hear at church.

3. As a result of this chapter and our discussion I will:

4. I will start on _____.

---

[1] I am thankful that Stevie and his family knew Christ. After I believed in Jesus we became close. We worshipped together and talked about "Neethus" as he named our Savior. I look forward to losing badly to him on the King's court.

[2] Thomas L. Constable, "Notes on Hebrews" (2015): 59.

[3] Constable, "Notes on Hebrews," 70–71.

[4] "What Were the Cities of Refuge in the Old Testament?," GotQuestions.Org, n.d., https://www.gotquestions.org/cities-of-refuge.html.

[5] Morris, Leon, *Hebrews*, vol. 12 of *The Expositor's Bible Commentary* (Grand Rapids: Zondervan, 1981), 61.

Chapter 9

He Is of a Better Order
(7:1-28)

Back in the late 1980's my wife and I were driving around 95 mph on the German autobahn in an area with no speed limit. I glanced in the left side–view mirror and saw headlights flash—an indication of a pass, but too far back to make out the car. Less than three or four seconds later a forest green 911 screamed past like a bullet train passing a bicycle. I literally lost my breath! That Porsche forcefully expressed its absurd superiority over the Volkswagen.

Our author "flashed his lights" when he previously mentioned Christ's high priestly ministry *in the order of Melchizedek*. Now he demonstrates from the Old Testament itself that it is a better priesthood. If Jesus is of a biblically better order, why return to Aaron's?

Four Old Testament verses (Gn 14:18-20; Ps 110:4) complete Melchizedek's story that Hebrews 7:1-3 summarizes. Who was this strange figure?

One view is that he was a Theophany—an Old Testament appearance of Christ. However, Psalm 110:4 and Hebrews 5:6 distinguish Him from Melchizedek; they are two different people. A second opinion sees him as an angel, but God requires a priest to be a human male (5:1).

The last interpretation, preferred here, is that Melchizedek was a historical person with no Biblical record of his parentage or death, which makes him appear to be eternal. Therefore, the writer uses Melchizedek to explain and illustrate Jesus' better priesthood. It is supreme for He is a more excellent person who makes supreme provision.

Jesus Is a Better Person (7:1-10)

It is not that Jesus is like Melchizedek; instead, Melchizedek is *made like the Son of God* (3). Genesis 14:18-20 is the backdrop as Abraham returns victorious from battle.

He Is Greater than Abraham (1-3)

(1–2) *Melchizedek* is the initial priest mentioned in the Bible. He is *King of Salem* [Jerusalem], *priest of the Most High God*, a King-Priest who ruled from Jerusalem as will Jesus. *By the translation of his name*, he is *king of righteousness, and then also. . . king of peace* just as Jesus will be (Ps 85:8–13; Zc 6:13; Lk 1:67–79).

Melchizedek met Abraham as he was returning from the slaughter of the kings and blessed him, to whom also Abraham apportioned a tenth part of all the spoils. In accepting his blessing and tithing to Melchizedek, Abraham recognized him as a spiritual superior. His royal priesthood was more excellent than Abraham's family priesthood. This superiority is discussed further in verses 4–7.

(3) Melchizedek is *without father, without mother, without genealogy, having neither beginning of days nor end of life, but made like the Son of God,* so it appears that *he remains a priest perpetually* just as Jesus does. His person and priesthood surpass Abraham.

He Is Greater than Aaron and Levi (4-10)

(4-6a) *Now observe how great this man was to whom Abraham the patriarch gave a tenth of the choicest spoils. Those indeed of the sons of Levi who receive the priest's office have commandment in the Law to collect a tenth from the people, that is, from their brethren, although these are descended from Abraham.*

The Levites received tithes from their equals by God's command, not personal superiority (Nm 18:21, 24–26). *But the one whose genealogy is not traced from them collected a tenth from Abraham* because he was greater in person.

(6b-7) Furthermore, he *blessed the one who had the promises.* Both men worshipped God Most High who had made covenant with Abraham. Still, Abraham accepted his blessing, acknowledging his superiority, for *without any dispute the lesser is blessed by the greater.*

(8-10) *Melchizedek's* greater order appears to continue with no death or succession, unlike that of Levi, for *in this case, mortal men receive tithes, but in that case, one receives them, of whom it is witnessed that he lives on.*

Levi descended from Abraham *and, so to speak, through Abraham even Levi, who received tithes, paid tithes, for he was still in the loins of his father when Melchizedek met him.*

Abraham begat Isaac who begat Jacob who begat *Levi*; thus, at that time *Levi* was seminally in Abraham's body. Levi's tithe through father Abraham validates *Melchizedek's* supreme priesthood.

Thus, *Melchizedek* illustrates that Jesus the eternal One is superior to *Abraham* and *Levi* in person and priestly authority.

Jesus Has a Better Priesthood (7:11-19)

Jesus is also supreme because His priesthood replaced the Levitical order.

It Is a Royal Priesthood (11-14)

(11–12) God's goal for the redeemed is *perfection*, to be like Christ and reign with Him forever. It could not come *through the Levitical priesthood* although they initiated and implemented the law system. *Perfection* demanded another priesthood and another founding principle, *for when the priesthood is changed, of necessity there takes place a change of law also*. Moses, a Levitical priest, mediated the law, so changing the priesthood demanded its replacement. Therefore, Jesus' priesthood *according to the order of Melchizedek* rests on something superior to the old covenant. It is Christ's new covenant, more fully developed in chapters eight and nine.

(13-14) The core requirement of an Aaronic high priest was a genealogy proving direct descent from Aaron (Ez 2:61-63; Nh 7:63-65). This legally separated the offices of king and priest, so neither Aaron nor his order could ever fill that role. However, Jesus could.

The one concerning whom these things are spoken belongs to another tribe, from which no one has officiated at the altar. For it is evident that our Lord was descended from Judah, a tribe with reference to which Moses spoke nothing concerning priests. Judah was the kingly tribe but never the priestly, but since Jesus is *from Judah* and of Melchizedek's order, He alone is the King-Priest.

It Is Empowered by Indestructible Life (15-17)

Now the author moves to Psalm 110:4 to show that it too speaks of another and better priesthood.

(15-17) *And this is clearer still, if another priest arises according to the likeness of Melchizedek, who has become such not on the basis of a law of physical requirement, but according to the power of an indestructible life. For it is attested of Him, "YOU ARE A PRIEST FOREVER ACCORDING TO THE ORDER OF MELCHIZEDEK."* Psalm 110:4 confirms the basis of Jesus' priesthood as resurrection life, not lineage through Aaron. His order is permanent as David predicted even while the Levitical order was operative. Hundreds of years before Jesus, God planned to replace the Aaronic high priests.

It Can Perfect (18-19)
(18-19) The author returns to his initial subject in this section, *perfection* (11). *For, on the one hand, there is a setting aside of a former commandment* [the entire law] *because of its weakness and uselessness (for the Law made nothing perfect).* On the other hand, Jesus' priesthood replaced it *with a bringing in of a better hope,* the confidence that He will enable maturity and bring us to His kingdom (3:6; 6:11, 18-19; 10:23). This assurance is the basis *through which we draw near to God* (4:16; 7:25; 10:22; 11:6). Jesus' royal, eternal priesthood that perfects cancels the need for Aaron's.

Jesus Makes Better Provision (7:20-28)
Chapter 5:1-10 summarized the purpose and character of the two priestly lines. This section repeats and expands that subject.

He Guarantees a New Covenant (20-22)
(20-21) God was silent at the installation of Aaron and his sons *for they indeed became priests without an oath*. He spoke to Moses about the priesthood but never to the priests. On the other hand, God swore directly to Christ, authorizing Him to operate eternally: THE LORD HAS SWORN AND WILL NOT CHANGE HIS MIND," YOU ARE A PRIEST FOREVER."

(22) By that oath *so much the more also Jesus has become the guarantee of a better covenant.* The *better covenant* enables new birth and spiritual growth, the subjects of chapter 8.

He Lives Forever to Save Forever (23-25)
(23) The Levitical priesthood was temporary because *the former priests, on the one hand, existed in greater numbers* being *prevented by death from continuing.* But Jesus, on the other hand, because He continues forever, holds His priesthood permanently.

(24-25) His unchanging priesthood *is able also to save forever* [Gk. completely]. Salvation once again speaks of kingdom deliverance, here from the power of sin. Jesus is the Priest-King who grows and rewards *those who draw near to God through Him* [4:16; 7:19; 10:22; 11:6] *because He always lives to make intercession for them.*

Jesus' intercession does not keep us eternally secure. Eternal security is bound up in partaking of God's life (eternal) and the faithfulness and truthfulness of the Godhead. Instead, the King-Priest-Son intercedes for our growth to a Father who always hears and grants His request. His promise and prayer for Peter during his test, failure, despair, and restoration illustrate his prayers for us, as does John 17.

His Character Is Perfect (26)
(26) Many of Aaron's descendants were excellent, faithful men while others were not. To bring us through our life struggles to the kingdom, we need a worthier priest, so *it was fitting* [Gk. appropriate] *for us to have such a high priest.*

Jesus is, was and ever will be the perfect One. *Holy* is spotlessness in words and works while *innocent* concerns pure attitudes and motives. *Undefiled* depicts His absolute purity. He has conquered the challenges of followership. *Separated from sinners* He is incorruptible. He sits *exalted above the heavens* to serve as our King-Priest. No Levitical priest could equal Him.

His Sacrifice Is Complete (27-28)
(27) Both daily and on the Day of Atonement, *the priest had to offer up sacrifices, first for His own sins and then for the sins of the people* (Ex 29:38-46; Lv 4:3-12; 16:6). Jesus *does not need* to offer an oblation for Himself or anyone or anything. *He did* [this] *once for all when He offered up Himself.* His single sacrifice terminated any need for the Levitical system and secured everything essential to endure.

(28) In summary, *the Law appoints men as high priests who are weak, but the word of the oath, which came after the Law, appoints a Son made perfect forever.*

So, Jesus' priesthood in the order of *Melchizedek* is greater than Aaron's and Levi's because He is a supreme person with a royal priesthood that can perfect believers. By an indestructible life, He replaces the priesthood and the law, secures the new covenant and saves forever. He offered the complete sacrifice and has a perfect character. He provides everything we need to train to reign. Why would anyone return to an incapable, invalid priesthood?

Positioning for Companionship

1. Share your major take-away from this chapter with your friend.

2. Jesus prays for our perfection. What are two things that you believe He regularly prays about for your growth? How can you tell that He does? What difference are His prayers making? Discuss this.

3. Because of this chapter and our discussion, I will:

4. I will start on _____.

Chapter 10

His Better Covenant
(8:1-13)

Do you like change? If so, you are rare. About 80 percent of people prefer status quo to change.[1]

People genuinely believe (often on an unconscious level) that when you've been doing something a particular way for some time, it must be a good way to do things. And the longer you've been doing it that way, the better it is.

In one study, people who saw a painting described as having been painted in 1905 found it far more pleasing to look at than people who saw the same painting described as created in 2005. In another, they admired the appearance of a tree described as being 4,500 years old more than did those who thought the same tree just 500 years old.

So, change isn't simply about embracing something unknown—it's about giving up something old (and therefore good) for something new (and therefore not good). The bottom line is, unconsciously we almost always believe that longevity = goodness.[2]

Such beliefs are even more ardent if God or religion is involved. Imagine the resistance to exchanging Judaism for Jesus. That's exactly what the Hebrews faced—the struggling transition from the 1500-year-old Jewish worship system led by the Aaronic high priest in the tabernacle and temple to Jesus as the invisible high priest in the heavenly sanctuary.

To help their transition, the author has carefully described Christ's high priesthood in five chapters. We might wonder, "What more can he say?"

But he has not yet explained how Jesus carries out his duties. Now, from 8:1-10:18 he unveils that Jesus has a superior ministry under a better covenant. He introduces and summarizes these two concepts in chapter eight.

Jesus Has a Better Ministry (8:1-5)

These verses summarize and repeat much of chapters 3-7.

He Serves from a Better Position (1)

(1) *Now the main point in what has been said is this: we have such a high priest who has taken His seat at the right hand of the throne of the Majesty in the heavens.* The Lord Jesus is superior because He is seated and enthroned in the heavens.

He Serves in a Better Place (2-5)

God appointed the priests, the offerings, and the place where they were to make sacrifices (Dt 12:8-14). Jesus excels in these areas too.

(2) He is *a minister* [Gk. sacred servant] *in the sanctuary and in the true tabernacle, which the Lord pitched, not man.* His sacrificial work done and installed as Priest-King, Christ constantly serves in the *true tabernacle* in heaven (7:15-22). The Aaronic high priests could only stand while serving once a year at the earthly throne of God, the mercy seat.

(3) *Every high priest is appointed to offer* [Gk. keep offering] *both gifts and sacrifices; so it is necessary that this high priest also have something to offer* [Gk. once]. Of course, Jesus sacrificed Himself once for all (7:27; 9:12, 28).

(4) *Now if He were on earth, He would not be a priest at all, since there are those who offer the gifts according to the Law.* As a descendant of Judah, He cannot qualify to serve in Aaron's tabernacle. Therefore, He attends in the heavenly tabernacle as a Melchizedekian priest.

(5) Perhaps in a vison or a scroll, God gave Moses a plan or blueprint of the heavenly tabernacle to build the earthly model (Ex 25:8–9, 40; 26:30; Nm 8:4; Ac 7:44). Thus, Aaron's place of ministry was only a *copy and shadow of the heavenly things* where Jesus serves.

The difference is rather like flying the genuine space shuttle compared to the best radio-controlled scale model on earth. Both operate, but the copy can never equal the original in function, form, or effect. To return to that system would be ineffective, unwise, and dangerous.

Jesus Mediated a Better Covenant (6-12)

(6) Jesus' ministry is *more excellent* because it is based on *a better covenant* that He mediated (7:12; 9:15; 12:24).

A mediator is one who intervenes between two estranged parties to reconcile them or to implement an act or agreement between them.

Moses mediated the inferior, conditional old covenant which promised blessings for perfect obedience. But Christ, in His own blood, *enacted* the more excellent new covenant *on better promises*.

Those better promises also include a better purpose than the law.

Its Better Purposes (7-8)

(6) To Replace the Old Covenant. We tend to picture the Ten Commandments and all the rules when we think of the law. However, its primary purpose and promises are found in Exodus 19:5-6:

> *'Now then, if you will indeed obey My voice and keep My covenant, then you shall be My own possession among all the peoples, for all the earth is Mine; and you shall be to Me a kingdom of priests and a holy nation.' These are the words that you shall speak to the sons of Israel.*

(7) The Law was Israel's national constitution, and this is the preamble. God intended covenant obedience to make Israel His select and precious *kingdom of priests, a holy nation* mediating the Lord to the nations. This did not happen *for if that first covenant had been faultless* [Gk. and it was not], *there would have been no occasion sought for a second.* The law is holy, spiritual and has a share of glory (Rm 7:12, 14; 2 Cr 3:7-11) but it simply could not prepare Israel for the kingdom. Unable to give eternal life, deliver from sin's rule or empower their faithfulness, it had to be replaced.

(8a) To Remake People. The people were also flawed, unable to keep the Law or become mature and kingdom ready. Commit as they would, they could not observe its core demand—**perfect** obedience (Ex 19:5, 8; 24:3, 7-8; Dt 5:27-29, 5:31-6:3; 11:22-23; 28:1).

Indeed, God promised the new covenant through Jeremiah because both the law and the people failed. *For finding fault with them, He says, "Behold, days are coming, says the Lord, When I will effect a new covenant with the house of Israel and with the house of Judah.*

The heart of the new covenant quoted here is Jeremiah 31:31-34. God promised it to Israel and Judah, a pair that usually refers to national Israel when used together. Since the new covenant is made with Israel alone, how can it apply to the church?

Additionally, there are 13 future tense verbs in verses 8-12. If it is yet future, how can the church be under the new covenant now?

> There are three general views: (1) the covenant is exclusively with Israel, (2) there are two covenants—one with Israel and one with the church, and (3) there is one covenant with a two-fold application—first promised to the Jews for the kingdom age and presently enjoyed by the church.[3]

The third view seems best. Jesus intends full physical and spiritual fulfillment for Israel in the millennium but makes partial spiritual application to the Church today, as does the Abrahamic covenant (Gl 3:6–4:7). This understanding takes the promises to Israel and Jesus' words to the church (Lk 22:20; 1 Cr 11:23-25) at face value. It maintains the Biblical distinction between Israel and the Church and fits the kingdom context of Hebrews.

The fulfillment of the New Covenant will be seen in two places: on earth, during the millennium and in the new heaven and earth for all eternity.

Its Better Promises (8:8b-13)

The new covenant's *better promises* include many physical blessings to Israel, but the author considers the spiritual benefits here.

New Covenant Promises to Israel

These gracious promises all relate to the nation's future spiritual life in the millennium. Then they will finally be God's kingdom of priests. The new covenant will:

- Be unconditional and all of grace—I will 7x (8–12)
- Be after those days—the Tribulation (8, 10a; Jr 31:27–30)
- Replace the Mosaic covenant—not like the covenant... (9)

- Regenerate the nation—put my laws into their minds... (10a)
- Give a unique relationship with God—My people (10b)
- Provide personal knowledge of God—all will know Me (11)
- Provide forgiveness—I will remember their sins no more (12)

What does the new covenant provide the church?

New Covenant Blessings to the Church

(8–10) We enjoy life under grace. Grace replaces the law as our new covenant rule of life (Rm 6:14). Now we relate with and serve God from acceptance rather than for it. Grace restrains sin and empowers us to live righteously (Rm 6:14-15). It enables our endurance so that we can inherit companionship (Hb 4:16).

(10b) We enjoy regeneration. The old covenant possessed neither life to give nor power to enable. In contrast, the new provides one with a new heart, mind, will and eternal life. New birth gives us entrance to the kingdom and enables us to train for companionship (Jn 3:3, 5; Ti 3:3-7). Regeneration restores our original capacities for fellowship, followership, and rulership.

(11) We enjoy personal knowledge of God. Belief in Jesus gives one eternal life (Jn 3:15-17). Jesus also said, *This is eternal life, that they may know You, the only true God, and Jesus Christ whom You have sent* (Jn 17:3). Eternal life is not just living forever; it is the opportunity (*may know*) to grow in the personal knowledge of God and Jesus endlessly, beginning now. Eternal life is a present, abundant quality of life that centers on fellowship with the Father and Son. Eternal life in the kingdom will include our everlasting roles and rewards.

(12) We enjoy forgiveness of sins and iniquities. The Law did not remove sins. It only covered them for a year at a time, and even then, not all sins. There was no provision for deliberate sins; just judgment. The new covenant does not cover sins; it removed them **all** forever (Jn 1:29; Rm 4:5–8)! God never recalls, records, or reminds us of them again—He even provides positional righteousness. What an astonishing contrast with the law.

(13) In conclusion, the writer reminds the readers that *when He said, "A new covenant," He has made the first obsolete.* Jeremiah's prediction of a new covenant over 500 years earlier indicated even then that God intended to replace the first covenant.

The author once worked in a Christian bookstore which had sold the best-selling Bible for decades. The publisher alerted management that a new edition of that translation was to be released some months out. We were to continue selling the old one until the release of the new, then we were to pull all the obsolete translations from the shelf and return them to the publisher. They would no longer be available, for the new would replace them.

When Jeremiah recorded the new covenant, Judaism was already *growing old.* As the author penned Hebrews, it was *ready to disappear,* likely a reference to the imminent devastation of Jerusalem in 70 A.D. The Hebrews must leave Judaism and remain separate from it. It was superseded and on the eve of destruction.

The new covenant is better than the old because it is enacted on better promises with better purposes by the better priest.

Positioning for Companionship

1. Share your major take–away from this chapter with your friend.

2. Which new covenant blessing has the most significant impact on your daily choices? In what way? How does it affect your relationship? Feelings? Talk with your friend about this.

3. Because of this chapter and our discussion, I will:

4. I will begin on

[1] Author: Richard Becker | Posted at: 6:00 AM | Filed Under: leadership et al., "If 80 Percent Of People Won't Change, Why Force Them?," n.d., http://www.richardrbecker.com/2014/03/if-80-percent-of-people-wont-change-why.html.

[2] Heidi Grant Halvorson Ph.D., "Explained: Why We Don't Like Change," *Huffington Post*, 5 November 2011, https://www.huffingtonpost.com/heidi-grant-halvorson-phd/why-we-dont-like-change_b_1072702.html.

[3] Ray Baughman, *The Kingdom of God Visualized* (Birmingham, AL: Shepherd Press, 1972), 62.

Chapter 11

His Better Ministries
(9:1-14)

The Winston's were an elderly couple participating in a church plant that rented a school building on Sundays. One morning they discovered that someone had thrown a brick through one of the exterior door windows.

Glass and debris lay scattered across the room. The couple was quite upset, and Mr. Winston warned, "Oh, whoever did that is in big trouble! This is God's house!"

We may call a church building God's house, but we know He doesn't live there. It's just a place to worship, serve and fellowship. Judaism was different. The tabernacle was God's actual dwelling so what the priests did and where they did it was critical.

The author continues to contrast Jesus' better ministry with Judaism. Here he shows that Christ provides for inner cleansing and intimacy with God that Judaism cannot.

The Old Covenant Ministry (9:1-10)

The old covenant ministry centered on the tabernacle with its divine directions. A reprise of the word *regulations, earthly, washings* and *body* (1, 10) sets this off. Perhaps using the tabernacle as his example emphasized the expiring nature of the old covenant. As a tent, it suggested impermanence and implied a need for replacement.

It's Services (1)

(1a) *Now even the first covenant had regulations of divine worship.* God gave the protocols for the priests for He will be worshiped as He determines, not by the inclinations and values of men. This is a subtle reminder to the Hebrews to draw near to Christ rather than the Temple.

It reminds us that worship is not about our preferred style of music, technology, or programs. That pretty much makes it about us and our preferences. These are not wrong, but authentic worship is God focused and man changing. Many saints search diligently for a church with a worship style they enjoy, while God searches for a specific type of worshipper (Jn 4:23–24).

It's Sanctuary (1-5)

(1b-2) *The earthly sanctuary or* tabernacle had a "split tent" form with two sections. The *outer one* was called the holy place, which symbolized heaven (24), inside of which *were the lampstand and the table and the sacred bread.*

(3) *Behind the second veil there was a tabernacle which is called the Holy of Holies* where God sat enthroned above the mercy seat and below the cherubim of glory (1 Sm 4:4; 2 Sm 6:2). Before the veil was the *altar of incense* on which the high priest burnt incense before the mercy seat on the annual Day of Atonement. The mercy seat was the top of the box itself.

(4) *The ark of the covenant* contained *a golden jar holding the manna and Aaron's rod which budded and the tables of the covenant.* These items represented God's faithful grace and Israel's wilderness apostasies. God provided food, the priesthood and the covenant. Israel rejected God's provision of manna (Nm 11), and the Aaronic priesthood (Nm 16) and repeatedly rebelled against His precepts.

(5) Simply noting the tabernacle furniture, the writer ignored the details.

It's Sacrifices (6-7)

(6-7) The Levitical sacrifices were limited for four reasons. The tabernacle was inaccessible to all but a select few, as only *priests* or *the high priest* could engage in the ministry. The presence of God was restricted whereas we are priests who can draw near.

No sacrifices were final as *they are continually entering the outer tabernacle performing the divine worship*. And on the annual Day of Atonement, unlike Jesus, the high priest must offer for himself before he can mediate for the people. *But into the second, only the high priest enters once a year, not without taking blood, which he offers for himself.*

Finally, the sacrifices were limited by their effect in that they only covered *the sins of the people committed in ignorance.*

It's Significance (8-10)

(8-9a) The import of this review of the inadequate earthly service is that th*e Holy Spirit is signifying this, that the way into the holy place* [God's presence] *has not yet been disclosed while the outer tabernacle is still standing, which is a symbol for the present time*. All that the tabernacle foreshadowed was unclear until after Christ completed His ministry. Then reality replaced the symbol that God no longer accepted.

(9b-10) For around 1500 years, hundreds of thousands of gallons of blood, forests of wood, thick columns of smoke, tons of burning fat and restricted access to the tabernacle suggested that the *gifts and* *sacrifices are offered which cannot make the worshiper perfect in conscience.* That system could only provide ceremonial, external cleansing, *since they relate only to food and drink and various washings, regulations for the body.* It set one apart physically but not spiritually. Nothing in Judaism could provide or promote intimacy with God.

God *imposed* this only *until a time of reformation* because He intended to replace it from the day it began. That reform or "new order of things" began with Jesus' death that mediated the new covenant.

The New Covenant Ministry (9:11-10:15)

Christ's ministry does provide for intimacy with God as the contrast discloses.

It's Better Services (11a)

(11a) *But when Christ appeared in heaven as a high priest of the good things to come* seems to refer to all the promised blessings that began with His exaltation and will be consummated in His kingdom. *To come* is likely an ingressive aorist, meaning "the good things that have now begun to come into existence."[1]

From justification to glorification, Jesus' priestly ministry provides and prepares believers for so much more to come in the kingdom.

It's Better Sanctuary (11b)

(11b) After His one-time sacrifice, the Lord *entered through the greater and more perfect tabernacle, not made with hands, that is to say, not of this creation.* Our King—Priest performs His ministry in heaven where He always sits in God's presence.

It's Better Sacrifice (12a-14)

(12) He entered *not through the blood of goats and calves, but through His own blood.* His sinless blood voided the need for any more Levitical offerings, for *He entered the holy place once for all.* Christ's sacrifice was better on several accounts. First, it was personal—He was the sacrifice. It was sinless human blood rather than that of an animal. Next, it was absolute rather than annual. Finally, it provided multiple spiritual effects, two of which are mentioned.

The first is *having obtained eternal redemption*. Some understand that Christ had to take His blood to the heavenly holy place to complete the sacrifice. However, when He arrived there, redemption was already finished—*having obtained*. It was finished on the cross (Jn 19:30).

The Old Testament uses *redemption* almost exclusively of temporal deliverance from problems or the provision of earthly blessings. On the other hand, the new covenant *eternal redemption* provides spiritual blessings. They include forgiveness (Ep 1:7), justification (Rm 3:24), adoption (Gl 4:5), the indwelling Spirit (Gl 3:13–14), power for sanctification (Ti 2:14), resurrection, kingdom glory (Rm 8:23; Ep 1:14) and inheritance (Ti 3:7; Hb 9:15).

(13-14) An additional blessing of Jesus' redemption is inner cleansing *for if the blood of goats and bulls and the ashes of a heifer sprinkling those who have been defiled sanctify for the cleansing of the flesh how much more will the blood of Christ who through the eternal Spirit offered Himself without blemish to God,* **cleanse your conscience** *from dead works*.

Rather than forcing Jesus to the altar as with an old covenant lamb or bull, the entire Trinity voluntarily provided Christ's sacrifice. The Father planned it, *the eternal Spirit* prompted it and flawless Jesus provided it.

Dead works are sacrifices and rituals that are *dead* in that they cannot cleanse within. Jesus' blood wipes the believer's conscience and inner person clean. It positionally releases from guilt and ought to liberate us from any sense of needing sacrifices for forgiveness.

Christ's offering frees believers *to* (Gk. continually) *serve the living God* as new covenant priests. Christ's offering provides His royal priests with the capacity to steadfastly serve, endure, and gain reward as they live in intimacy with God and a clean conscience.

We do not need to withdraw to Judaism or in our day, ritualism, tradition or the centrality of professional clergy. Jesus and the new covenant are preeminent.

The Superiority of Christ's New Covenant Service Hb 9:1-15	
Old Covenant Inferiority	**New Covenant Superiority**
Earthly (1)	Heavenly (11)
A copy (2-5, 8-9, 23-24)	The reality (11-12; 23-24)
Continual sacrifices (6-9a)	Final sacrifice (12)
Multiple sacrifices (6-7)	One sacrifice (11-14)
Multiple priests (6-7)	One priest (11)
Unintentional sins only (7)	Transgressions also (15)
Incomplete (9b)	Complete (12)
External and temporary (10, 13)	Internal and eternal (14)

Positioning for Companionship

1. Share your major take–away from this chapter with your friend.

2. Describe any struggles you have with false guilt or failure to serve. Try to define the cause of any issue and prepare a replacement strategy. Work together on this with your companion. If you don't have a problem, spend some time thanking the Lord together and pray for someone you know who may struggle.

3. Because of this chapter and our discussion, I will:

4: I will start on:

---

[1] Morris, Leon, *Hebrews*, vol. 12 of *The Expositor's Bible Commentary* (Grand Rapids: Zondervan, 1981), 89.

Chapter 12

The Effects of His Better Sacrifice (9:15-10:18)

If necessity is the mother of invention, then repetition is the father of learning. Toddlers learn to talk by hearing words repeated, identifying them with certain people, things or events and mimicking the sounds. PGA players hit a thousand balls a day to hone their skills. How did you learn to drive? By driving, parking, and braking time after time. Surely God has repeated some lessons in your Christian life. We must hear and do things frequently to progress.

To conclude his exposition of Jesus' priesthood our author restates the measureless nature and effects of His sacrifice on believers.

It Mediated A New Covenant (9:15-22)

(15) *For this reason He is the mediator of a new covenant, so that, since a death has taken place for the redemption of the transgressions that were committed under the first covenant, those who have been called may* *receive the promise of the eternal inheritance. For this reason,* connects back to the Lord's death in verses 12-14.

Covenant means both a human will and a covenant with God in this passage. Whereas we meet with lawyers, ancients ratified them in various ways. They exchanged sandals (Ru 4:7), mixed salt (2 Ch 13:5), shook hands (Ez 10:19) or shed animal blood (Gn 15:9-21). In a blood covenant, the animal sacrificed was a substitute for the one(s) making it, known as "cutting covenant," as a knife shed the blood.

(16-17) *For where a covenant* [human will] *is, there must of necessity be the death of the one who made it. For a covenant is valid only when men are dead, for it is never in force while the one who made it lives.* In either a human will or a covenant with God, someone or something must die before anyone receives the inheritance.

(18-21) *Therefore, even the first covenant was not inaugurated without blood.* Three things occurred to initiate the Law. First, Moses explained it: *for when every commandment had been spoken by Moses to all the people according to the Law,* and second, *he sprinkled both the book itself and all the people, saying, "This is the blood of the covenant which God commanded you."* Finally, *in the same way he sprinkled both the tabernacle and all the vessels of the ministry with the blood.*

(22) *And according to the Law one may almost say, all things are cleansed with blood.* God graciously allowed some of the poor who could not afford animals to bring a flour offering in place of an animal if they could not afford two doves (Lv 5:11-13). He would consider it an animal, for the principle is *without shedding of blood there is no forgiveness.*[1]

It Provided Complete Cleansing (9:23–24)

(23a) *All things* in verse 22 encompass every person, place, and utensil of the tabernacle. Sin contaminated everything so everything needed routine cleansing by blood. *Therefore, it was necessary for the copies of the things in the heavens* [earthly tabernacle] *to be cleansed with these* [animal sacrifices] *but the heavenly things themselves with better sacrifices than these.* Why did Christ's heavenly place of ministry need purging? Was heaven contaminated? J. Dwight Pentecost offers one possibility:

> Since earthly things needed cleansing, and they are copies of heavenly things, it corresponds that the heavenly things need cleansing. Further, it is clear from various passages that the heavens are not clean (Jb 4:18; 15:15; 25:5). It is also clear that when Adam sinned that defilement extended beyond the earth to the heavens, so that they need cleansing (Co 1:20). This is why all creation is awaiting its redemption (Rm 8:19-22). Thus Christ as the high priest not only appeared in the presence of God for us, but he also appeared to provide cleansing for "the heavenly things."[2]

Warren Wiersbe understands the cleansing differently.

> Certainly nothing in heaven is defiled in a literal sense, for sin cannot pollute the sanctuary of God. But, for that matter, nothing in the earthly tabernacle was literally defiled by sin. It all had to do with people's relationship to God. The blood sprinkled on a piece of furniture did not change the nature of that piece, but it changed God's relationship to it. God could enter into communion with people because of the sprinkled blood.[3]

Whatever the meaning, Jesus washed the heavenly original, allowing believers unhindered access to God.

(23b) What about *with better sacrifices than these*? Why plural *sacrifices* to cleanse heaven? It's likely a generic plural, using the plural to emphasize that sacrifice was *necessary* to purge the heavenly things (16, 23).[4]

(24) The sacrifices were better because God provided Christ to die, who then rose, ascended, and entered *into heaven itself*. Once there, God affirmed the completed value of His blood when He seated

Christ at His right hand, *now to appear in the presence of God for us as our great high priest.*

It Consummated Salvation (9:25-28)

After God accepted the sacrifices on the Day of Atonement, the high priest exited the tabernacle to announce to the people that their sins were covered. This consummated God's annual covering for sin. The author employs multiple terms to emphasize the single, eternal, concluding work of Jesus that far exceeds that of the Day of Atonement. Note *often* (25-26), *once* (26, 27, 28), *consummation* (26) and *put away* (26).

(25–26) *Nor was it that He would offer Himself often, as the high priest enters the holy place year by year with blood that is not his own. Otherwise, He would have needed to suffer often since the foundation of the world; but now once* [for all time] *at the consummation of the ages,* the last days (1:2) that were initiated by Christ's death.

He has been manifested to put away sin [singular, that is, the sin nature] *by the sacrifice of Himself.* Scripture uses the Greek term translated *put away* only once again, in 7:18, where it means to "legally annul." Jesus' death dissolved the legal authority of our sin nature.

Verse 28 reveals that Christ [was] *offered once to bear the sins of many.* *Sins* (plural) refers to individual sins. Jesus removed the sin (singular) of the world (Jn 1:29) when He died for the world–all people–not the "world of the elect." The singular sin indicates the sin nature.

People do not perish because of their sin. Jesus legally dealt with both their sin nature and their sins through His death and resurrection. People perish because they do not believe in Him (Jn 3:16-17). The *many* are those who believe in Him. *Many* does not refer to an elect group.

The Day of Atonement **covered** such sins but could not remove them nor do anything with the sin nature or the conscience. In contrast, Jesus dealt with the root (sin), the fruit (sins) and the product of sin (guilty consciences).

(27) *It is appointed for men to die once and after this comes judgment.* Jesus will judge all who do not believe in Him at the Great White Throne where their works will determine the severity of their eternal punishment (Rv 20:11–15). Works will not demonstrate if they are saved; that is settled in this life and sealed forever by simple belief in Jesus. Though works are a critical part of the Christian life and future rewards they do not demonstrate if we are saved or not. As Hebrews shows, believers can, and sometimes do, depart from Christ.

Believers in Jesus will not be judged at the Great White Throne. We will have been previously assessed at the Judgment Seat to determine our eternal rewards and roles based upon our works.

(28) As in the high priest's concluding announcement on the Day of Atonement, *so Christ also, having been offered once to bear the sins of many* [who believe in Him], *will* [leave the heavenly sanctuary to] *appear a second time for salvation without reference to sin, to those who eagerly await Him.* At this *salvation*, the Rapture, Jesus will save His church from the earth and its accompanying trials, temptations and enemies. He will not deal with sin for He has already done so.

All believers will go to be with Him, but only *those who eagerly await Him*, who have remained diligently faithful to Him, will enjoy full inheritance and companionship. The verse mentions only loyal believers to motivate the Hebrews to endure.[5]

Israel's high priest made three appearances on the Day of Atonement. Our high priest has three appearances. *He has been manifested to put away sin by the sacrifice of Himself* (26). *He now appear*[s] *in the presence of God for us* (24) and in the future, He *will appear a second time* (28). Interestingly, the uses of *appear* and *manifested* provide an outline of the book.[6]

Christ's Appearings and Hebrews Structure		
Has Appeared (26)	Is Appearing (24)	Will Appear (28)
Chapters 1-2	Chapters 3:1-10:18	Chapters 10:19-13:25
On the earth	In the heavens	In the air to the earth
To die	To pray	To reign
As Son-King	As Priest-King	As King-Priest-Son
So, we eagerly await Him!		

To Enable Sanctification (10:1-18)

The writer now further demonstrates how Jesus' better blood enables the sanctification and maturity of new covenant believers.

It Provides Positional Sanctification (1-10)

(1) Jesus' death puts away sin and sins, making maturity or perfection possible for believers today. This could not happen under the law. *For the Law, since it has only a shadow of the good things to come and not the very form of things, can never, by the same sacrifices which they offer continually year by year, make perfect those who draw near. Make perfect* does not mean to make sinless, but to grow up. The law could not because it had no substance to deal with sin; it was a mere shadow.

(2-3) *Otherwise, would they not have ceased to be offered, because the worshipers, having once been cleansed, would no longer have had consciousness of sins? But in those sacrifices there is a reminder of sins year by year.* One must enjoy a clear conscience to steadily mature. Persistent guilt paralyzes the inner person and steals confidence before God. It creates fear and a sense of defeat, which is what the law offerings did for worshippers.

(4-5a) The old covenant system was useless to save or sanctify *for it is impossible for the blood of bulls and goats to take away sins.* The author quotes Psalm 40:6-8 to remind the readers of Jesus' incarnation and its better, sanctifying sacrifice. *Therefore, when He comes into the world, He says,*

> SACRIFICE AND OFFERING YOU HAVE NOT DESIRED, BUT A BODY YOU HAVE PREPARED FOR ME; IN WHOLE BURNT OFFERINGS AND SACRIFICES FOR SIN YOU HAVE TAKEN NO PLEASURE. THEN I SAID, "BEHOLD, I HAVE COME (IN THE SCROLL OF THE BOOK IT IS WRITTEN OF ME) TO DO YOUR WILL, O GOD."

(5b) The Holy Spirit directed the writer to insert A BODY YOU HAVE PREPARED FOR ME in place of the original, MY EARS YOU HAVE BORED. This change highlights Jesus' enduring submission to the will of God as a man. To bore the ear was to mark willing obedience to a master for life (Ex 21:6; Dt 15:17). Jesus voluntarily became a man to do God's will in life and through death. He is ever the model of obedient endurance regardless of cost.

(6–7) Why did Jesus offer Himself? First, animal SACRIFICE AND OFFERING God has NOT DESIRED. Second, A BODY YOU HAVE PREPARED FOR ME as a sacrifice and third, God takes pleasure in obedience rather than WHOLE BURNT OFFERINGS. Therefore, HE SAID, "BEHOLD I HAVE COME TO DO YOUR WILL, O GOD. "

(8-10) Two results followed Jesus' incarnation and death. *He takes away the first* [old covenant] *in order to establish the second* [the new]. *And by this will we have been* [positionally] *sanctified through the offering of the body of Jesus Christ once for all.*

The term *will* may refer to Jesus' choice of obedience to God's will (7, 9) or to the new covenant (9). This commentary prefers the latter. Either way Jesus positionally sanctified believers forever.

He Enables Practical Sanctification (10:11-18)

Jesus' sacrifice also delivers experiential sanctification and endurance.

(11-13) *Every priest stands daily ministering and offering time after time the same sacrifices, which can never take away sins; but He, having offered one sacrifice for sins for all time,* completed His redemptive work and SAT DOWN AT THE RIGHT HAND OF GOD in His sanctifying work as great High Priest. He now anticipates His reign, *waiting from that time onward UNTIL HIS ENEMIES ARE MADE A FOOTSTOOL FOR HIS FEET.*

(14) As He waits, Jesus trains His people to reign with Him. *By one offering He has perfected for all time those who are sanctified* includes both positional and practical perfection. *Has perfected* is a tense indicating completed perfection; it is positional. *Are sanctified* should be translated "are being sanctified" because of its tense. It speaks to practical, progressive growth.

We experience sanctification as we daily heed His word (2:1-4), look to the kingdom (2:5-18), believe and labor for His promised rest (3:1-4:13), draw near to His throne (4:14-16), and diligently grow and endure (5:12-6:20).

(15-17) To verify this, *the Holy Spirit also testifies* [Gk. continuously] *to us* through the Scriptures. The writer restates two new covenant blessings: regeneration (16) and forgiveness (17). A new nature enables us to grow while forgiveness provides inner cleansing and confidence.

(18) Because of Jesus' accomplished work, *there is no longer any offering for sin* needed for a man or provided by the law. The readers must remain true to Jesus.

Christ's one—time sacrifice provides forgiveness, inner cleansing, and the power to grow and pursue kingdom rewards. Indeed, it is beyond better; it is the best!

The priesthood was the heart of Israelite worship. The author devoted the most extended section of his book to demonstrate its shortfalls. He showed that Jesus' definitive royal priesthood, new covenant and sacrifice put way both sin and sins forever, enabling sanctification and inheritance. Not Judaism but Jesus!

Positioning for Companionship

1.   Share your major take–away from this chapter with your friend.

2. The old covenant sacrifices reminded the people of their sins. What reminders do you find in your daily life that you are a sinful creature?[7] How can you respond to these with Christ's new covenant sacrifice?

3. As a result of this chapter and our discussion I will:

4: I will start on:

---

[1] Thomas L. Constable, "Notes on Hebrews" (2015): 97.

[2] J. Dwight Pentecost, *Faith That Endures: A Practical Commentary on the Book of Hebrews*, Revised Edition. (Grand Rapids: Kregel, 2002), 1471.

[3] Warren W. Wiersbe, *Be Confident* (Colorado Springs, CO: David C. Cook, 1982), 105.

[4] Morris, Leon, *Hebrews*, vol. 12 of *The Expositor's Bible Commentary* (Grand Rapids: Zondervan, 1981), 91.

[5] Joseph Dillow, *The Reign of the Servant Kings* (Miami Springs, FL: Schoettle Publishing Co., 1992), 129.

[6] Wiersbe, *Be Confident*, 107.

[7] Wiersbe, *Be Confident*, 166.

Section 3

Companions Train to Reign With the King
(10:19-13:25)

Hebrews concludes with encouragement to put the greatness of Christ's word and work into practice. Potential companions must remain faithful priests (10:9-39), seek rewards by faith (11:1-40) and accept adversity as training for rulership (12:1-13). As a household of royal priests, they are to protect, obey, love, serve and worship together (12:14-13:25). Persevering practice of this section is the path to partnership.

Chapter 13

Warning: Be Faithful Priests
(10:19-39)

One of the longest days of my life occurred in an eighth-grade spring football game. I was a defensive lineman and loved it. Back then football was primarily a run game; we only threw the ball seven or eight times a game. Pretty much my whole job was to run into, over or through offensive linemen on the other team and break the ball carrier into small pieces. Fire off and smack down. It was fabulous.

Sometime in the second half, coach told me to play left defensive end which I had never done and knew little about except that I was too slow. On the first snap the ball carrier came my way, so I did what a D lineman always did—blitzkrieg. Bad move. A defensive end needs to hang back a count or so to turn the runner in. The running back cut outside me for a big gain. The same thing happened the next two plays. That's when I heard coach screaming,

"Play your position! Play your position! Play your position!" Those three words still ring true: play your position.

This fourth warning can easily fit with 3:1-10:18 or 11:1-13:25 as it transitions between the priestly and practical sections of the book. Practical application of Christ's priesthood means that the brothers are to play their position as a house of priests.

As a Middle Eastern, Old Testament based book, Hebrews underscores community and corporate life, not individualism. We are responsible to help each other endure.

The term *confidence* (19, 35) ties the warning together, urging bold, faithful exercise as priests in community. Interestingly, verses 19-25 employ the triad of faith, hope and love while verses 32-29 illustrate and encourage expressions of faith, hope and love.

Stimulate One Another (10:19-25)

Therefore brethren introduces two reasons to encourage and protect one another.

(19-20) First, we can hearten one another *since we have confidence* [Gk. freedom of speech] *to enter the holy place by the blood of Jesus*. Our confident access *is by a new and living way which He inaugurated for us through the veil, that is, His flesh.*

The tabernacle veil kept everyone, priests, and people, from God's presence except for one man once a year. When Jesus' died, the veil of the temple was torn apart from top to bottom (Mt 27:51; Mk 15:38; Lk 23:45). This vividly symbolized *new* [Gk. fresh] access to God via Jesus' body and blood. The old priesthood and its restrictions are dead. God's presence is open to any believer, anytime. It is *living* as well because the new covenant functions by the power of an indestructible life (7:16). Why return to a system that keeps you hopelessly locked out?

(21) Second, we can incite mutual perseverance *since we have a great priest* whose preeminence resides in His character, appointment, and order, His covenant, and His ministry (3:1-10:18). He not only ministers to us, but He also leads us for He is *over the house of God*.

Based on these privileges of sure access and exalted leadership, the author urges the readers to faithfulness in three priestly roles. With a threefold use of *let us,* and 15 plurals, he is quick to emphasize life together.

Let Us Draw Near in Prayer: Faith (22)

(22) Every believer has the privilege of prayer but the emphasis here is *let **us** draw near*. We are to pray individually and together with *a sincere heart in full assurance* [confidence that we are guilt-free] *of faith, having our hearts sprinkled clean from an evil conscience.* Moses sprinkled the bodies of the defiled people with animal blood to cleanse them and to inaugurate the Law (9:13-14, 19). In contrast, the new covenant blood of Jesus has permanently purified us within, so we pray with certainty. *Having our bodies washed with pure water* likely refers to the response of a good conscience at water baptism (1 Pt 3:21), or possibly it is a figure of speech for regeneration (Ek 36:25).

Individual prayer is critical but confident corporate prayer was the norm in the early church (Ac 1:14; 2:42; 3:1; 6:4, 6; 12:5, 12; 16:13, 25; 21:5). Remarkable things occur when praying with others. It is a marvelous way to learn to pray, to gain sureness in asking, and to draw and give strength to others who struggle with similar challenges. Corporate prayer is one position a household of priests must play to remain faithful.

Let Us Hold Fast Our Confession: Hope (23)

(23) The writer repeats the core challenge of the book: *Let us hold fast the confession of our hope without wavering.* The context indicates that hope is a confident expectation rather than a "hope so." It rests in Christ's sufficiency, focuses on His return and kingdom and should motivate us to endurance.

Our loyalty rests on Christ's character, *for He who promised is faithful* and will deliver the loyal ones to the promised inheritance when He comes.

Let Us Encourage One Another: Love (24-25)

(24) Discouragement is always near at hand, especially when you've suffered long. When the load is heavy we all need someone to cheer us on or to help us carry it. We must *consider* or "set the mind" on (3:1) supporting one another. Rather than *forsaking our own assembling together*, we must engage it. *Assembling* is a unique form of the word synagogue, our own type of synagogue. It is no longer Jewish; instead, it is Jesus' new covenant house of royal priests.

The author loved his readers and empathized with their pressures. He felt similar stresses, so between the lines his heart cried out, "Let's be encouraged and press on together."

Priesthood is not about attending church services; it concerns hands—on helping each other become companions. Let's not just go into a building, sing some songs, hear a sermon, give an offering, and leave (but by all means, go!). Instead, let us ponder how we can rouse a brother to love and good deeds and then do it. When it truly grabs us, Hebrews will transform how we do church.

(25) Some understand *the day drawing near* to refer to Rome's coming destruction of Jerusalem in 70 A.D. It may be, but it may also mean the judgment seat of Christ (4:12-13; 9:28; 10:37). Either one ought to prompt mutual care.

Avoid Willful Sin Together (10:26-31)

The opposite of persevering priesthood is intentional withdrawal from Christ and the fellowship. That is willful sin. This sin receives a terrible response from God. The author uses several old covenant texts to explain why *(for)* we must remain steadfast priests and why God judges willful sin so severely.

Willful Sin Is Distinct (26-28)

(26a) None of the Hebrews are locked in to such a state *for if we go on sinning willfully* (Gk. maybe we will, perhaps we won't). *Willfully* reminds from Numbers 15:30-31 that covenant rejection is blasphemy and God's response was capital punishment.

> *But the person who does anything defiantly, whether he is native or an alien, that one is blaspheming the Lord; and that person shall be cut off from among His people. Because he has despised the word of the Lord and has broken His commandment, that person shall be completely cut off; His guilt will be on him.* (Nm 15:30-31)

(26b-27) For those who return to Judaism *there no longer remains a sacrifice for sins but a terrifying expectation of judgment*. The law provides no sacrifice to deter God's temporal wrath against willful covenant rejection. If a Hebrew saint returned to the Jewish system, he or she returned to a religion with no capacity to deal with their scenario.

This sin is so great that the old covenant offers only one consequence: being cut off, which is physical death. That is why the author quotes Isaiah 26:11, *and* THE FURY OF A FIRE WHICH WILL CONSUME THE ADVERSARIES. God treats believers who apostatize as if they are His enemies, for that is how they act.

(28) *Anyone who has set aside the Law of Moses* [by idolatry] *dies without mercy on the testimony of two or three witnesses* alludes to Deuteronomy 17:2-6 and capital punishment for idolatry.

The distinct, willful sin of Hebrews is deliberate blasphemy and idolatry by retreating to Judaism. It is worthy of death.

Willful Sin Is More Severely Judged (29-31)

Now the writer considers the new covenant punishment compared to the old.

(29a) He argues from the lesser to the greater. As stated in the previous verse, *if anyone who has set aside the Law of Moses* [rejected the old covenant] *dies without mercy* [capital punishment], *how much severer punishment do you think he will deserve* who rejects Jesus.

(29b) *He has trampled under foot the Son of God* or mocked and scorned Him as did many at His trials and crucifixion (Lk 22:63-65; 23:11, 35-37). Such a one *has regarded as unclean* [Gk. common, no different than animal blood!] *the blood of the covenant by which he was sanctified.* Finally, *he has insulted the Spirit of grace,* by whom Jesus offered Himself (9:14). This is to treat the Holy Spirit just as Israel's fathers did and reject His grace (Nh 9:30; Is 63:10; Ac 7:51). This description echoes and expands 6:6.

(30-31) God's character (*for we know Him*) demands that He respond consistently toward His idolatrous people under the new covenant. It is He *who said, "VENGEANCE IS MINE, I WILL REPAY." And again, "THE LORD WILL JUDGE HIS PEOPLE"* (Dt 32:35-36). Clearly directed at believers, this inescapable judgment is doubly terrifying, both in its expectation (27) and its execution (31), for *it is a terrifying thing to fall into the hands of the living God.*

The warning has direct application only to the Jewish—Christian generation who received it before the fall of Jerusalem. Indirectly it applies to us even though we are not tempted to return to Judaism.

Physical death was the old covenant penalty. We would face more severe punishment. Physical death is bad enough for it would end our opportunity to serve and endure. Even worse, at the Judgment Seat we could gain rewards only for works done before defection. Such eternal forfeitures would last forever which is far, far worse than physical death alone.

Endure by Faith Together (10:32-39)

Since the Hebrews had not committed this willful sin, the author strengthens their resolve to persevere.

Recall Your Past Endurance (32-34)

(32-33) He urges them to recall their past acceptance of short-term trouble for eternal treasure. *But remember the former days, when, after being enlightened, you endured a great conflict of sufferings, partly by being made a public spectacle through reproaches and tribulations, and partly by becoming sharers with those who were so treated. For you showed sympathy to the prisoners and accepted joyfully the seizure of your property.*

(34) How did they endure earlier losses of possessions, public ostracism and humiliation so well? They knew that *you have for yourselves a better possession and a lasting one* including the eternal city and the inheritance that can accompany it (11:10; 12:22).

Kingdom possessions and rewards will last forever in a culture of unending acceptance, love, and pleasure so we can release such things now to retain them permanently. The Hebrews did it once; they can do it again. The pressures may have changed but the promised prize has not.

Rely on God's Promises (35-39)

(35-36) Mentioning a secure, bountiful future prompted another challenge to persistent faith. *Therefore, do not throw away your confidence which has a great reward. For you have need of endurance, so that when you have done the will of God* [suffering and persevering] *you may receive what was promised*, inheritance and companionship.

(37) In a day of imminent national judgment by a vile people, God told Habakkuk to trust Him and wait on Messiah's promised coming and restoration (Is 26:20; Hk 2:3-4). This demanded patient faith in God's person and program FOR YET IN A VERY LITTLE WHILE, HE WHO IS COMING WILL COME, AND WILL NOT DELAY.

As with Habakkuk, the Hebrews also needed to trust Messiah to deliver them in His time. The present time of needed endurance is "short time" if we peer into eternity for the returning One.

(38-39a) *But my righteous one shall live by faith* could more accurately be translated here as "faithfulness." On the other hand, IF HE SHRINKS BACK [apostatizes], MY SOUL HAS NO PLEASURE IN HIM [now or at the judgment seat].

However, the author affirms, *we are not of those who shrink back* [fall away] *to destruction.* The word *destruction* can mean eternal judgment, but it need not in every instance. It and a related term are also translated *perish* (Ac 8:20) or *waste* (Mt 26:8; Mk 14:4). The author may be inferring that disavowing Christ leads to bodily destruction as temporal judgment, but it seems wise to see the meaning as a wasted life given the kingdom. To paraphrase, "We are not of those who fall away and waste our one opportunity to gain companionship."

The pressures on the Hebrews were going to increase so the writer warns them a fourth time of the grave temporal and eternal dangers of willfully departing from Christ and His priestly people. None had gone so far, but to obstinately repudiate Jesus and the church and return to Judaism would incur horrific judgment. To prevent such, he encourages them to patiently run together as a household of priests by faith in Jesus' promised return and rewards. The next chapter will illustrate that faith life.

Positioning for Partnership

1.   Share your major take–away from this chapter with your friend.

2.   Consider your relationships at church. Who needs encouragement? How can you blow some fresh air into their sail? Think back over your Christian life. Who has been a consistent encourager to follow Christ? Write them a thank you note.

3. As a result of this chapter and our discussion I will;
4. I will start on:

Chapter 14

Companions Seek Kingdom Rewards
(11:1-40)

Have you done the "trust fall?" A person standing with arms crossed over their chest deliberately falls backward, relying on others to catch them. Some people enjoy the rush while most are uncomfortable. After all, you give up any semblance of control that you may have. You've got to overcome the fear that you might get hurt. What if the catcher isn't strong enough to hold you or what if he slips? Or moves away?

A trust fall demands that you put confidence in someone who is behind you—invisible—rather than evident before you. Instead of trusting the invisible God and pressing on to His unseen reward, some of the Hebrews were returning to what they could see, the system of temple priests and sacrifices.

The author concluded chapter 10 by pointing them to *faith* or "living by faithfulness" as a core component of enduring to reward. Now he offers uplifting Old Testament models of such conviction to encourage the Hebrews to do likewise.

A Description of Faith (11:1-3)

The chapter describes enduring faith; it does not define it. It pictures what faith in the rewarding God **ought** to do in believers rather than what it **will** necessarily do. It ought to prompt steadfastness, but Hebrews has repeatedly indicated that believers do not always persevere until the end.

The behaviors of these Old Testament models of endurance do not prove they were saved; **their deeds prove they were seeking God and His rewards** (6).

Faith is always persuasion, confidence or belief based on available evidence that someone or something is true.[1] However, faith can differ in its objects and outcomes.

Saving faith is when an unbeliever becomes convinced that Jesus gives eternal life (Jn 3:16; 11:25-26; 1 Tm 1:16). This makes one a believer and provides kingdom entrance (Jn 3:2, 5).

The enduring faith of Hebrews 11 is when saints are persuaded *that God is and that He rewards those who seek Him.* Therefore, they steadfastly pursue Him and His rewards. Such faith pleases Him and makes one a companion. Thus, our diligent faith determines much of our kingdom experience.

Types of Faith			
Text	Type	Object	Outcomes
Jn 3:16	Saving Faith	Jesus	Eternal life, kingdom entrance
Hb 11:6	Enduring Faith	God and His promised rewards	Please God, rewarded kingdom experience

The author begins by mentioning three fundamentals of persevering faith.

Enduring Faith Acts on God's Promises (1)
(1) The Greek term *faith* appears 24 times in the chapter.[2] Twenty-three of the 24 express a persevering faith that looks to future reward.

The author first describes *faith* [as] *the assurance* [confidence or persuasion; 3:14; 10:38] *of things hoped for*.

Note the repetition of *things*. The *things* promised to the faithful are real items in the kingdom. We believe that they are genuine and literal and so act to gain them.

Such things include God's verbal approval (5, 6, 9), general rewards (6), heirship (7), inheritance of land (8), a city in the heavens (10), a heavenly country (13-16), treasure (26) and a better resurrection (35).

It is also the *conviction* [evidence] *of things not seen*. Such *conviction* demonstrates itself in actions. Every example in the chapter displayed an energetic belief in the future realities.

Belieivng Jesus for eternal life may or may not show up in one's acts, although it should. However, the enduring faith that seeks God's approval and His reward will consistently appear in actions.

We might contextually paraphrase as "Faith is an active confidence that things yet future and unseen will happen as God has revealed they will."

This vital concept runs right through the chapter: faith walkers know that kingdom things are more tangible and valuable than earthly things and so pursue them.

Enduring Faith Gains God's Approval (2)
(2) Such belief is how *the men of old gained approval* [Gk. received a witness] from God (10:38; 11:4-5, 39). He affirmed and rewarded the

quality of their lives because of their persevering trust. God's approval by faith opens and closes the chapter (1-2; 39).

Enduring Faith Embraces God's Viewpoint (3)
(3) Faith perceives that the visible *worlds* [Gk. ages] came from the invisible *word*. One cannot see the spoken *word of God*, yet we believe that it produced all that is, visible and invisible.

Ages refer to God preparing the flow of history as in 1:2. He designed history to unroll to His kingdom. This is true of nations, families, and our individual lives. It is an empowering comfort to believe that God designed our circumstances to direct and develop us for the kingdom.

People of steadfast faith perceive today through lenses tinted by the eternal tomorrow. Their values, goals, decisions, practices, and pursuits reflect the "opposite world."[3]

Faith Before the Flood (11:4-7)
Abel: Faith Worships Even When Persecuted (4)
(4) *Abel,* like the readers, had a *better sacrifice* but was persecuted by his brother for worshipping correctly. Those who based their hope of God's acceptance on an inferior sacrifice, like those in Judaism, would meet His rejection and punishment, as did *Cain*. Believers who suffered persecution from their Jewish brothers for trusting the better sacrifice of Christ would receive God's approval and continue to speak after their death as *Abel* did.[4]

Enoch: Faith Lives Righteously (5-6)
(5) Even though Abel died violently, Enoch did not die at all for God is master of death and life. *By faith Enoch was taken up so that he would not see death; AND HE WAS NOT FOUND BECAUSE GOD TOOK HIM UP.* Why did God exempt him from death and remove him? *For he obtained the witness* [from God] *that before his being taken up he was pleasing to God.*

How did Enoch please God for three centuries in that pernicious pre—flood world? God had revealed the second coming and maybe more to Enoch (Jd 1:14-15). He believed it, drew near the Lord, and looked away to Christ's return while demonstrating and declaring a righteous witness. This pleased the Lord.

(6) Abel and Enoch show that *without faith it is impossible to please Him, for he who comes* [Gk. draws near; 4:16, 7:25; 10:22] *to God must believe the He is and that He is a rewarder of those who seek Him.* Note that the message is to those who draw near—believers who act on His kingdom provision.

Those who walk for the opposite world believe three things about God. That He is; that He expects believers to seek Him; and that He rewards those who do.

He is may mean that God exists or that He is present and involved. The latter view seems best in the context of Hebrews.

Seek is present tense—ongoing and diligent like that of Enoch. Those tempted to fall away must realize this and press forward.

The Greek term *rewarder* marries two business words to paint a portrait of God. He "pays wages" (Gk. *misthos*; Mt 20:8; 1 Tm 5:8) and "reimburses" (Gk. *apodidomai*; Lk 10:35). God will pay His faithful people for our service and repay us for expenses or losses incurred in following Christ. There really will be an actual, literal payday someday!

Persevering after Christ is a gain—gain process. Although it costs much, maybe even life, we now gain the present joy and fullness of the abundant life. That leads to the second gain. The King will restore and multiply in the life to come all that it costs us. What grace!

God will reward us because it is one of His attributes. He is love, so He loves. He is true, so He cannot lie. He is a *rewarder*, so He rewards.

We please the Lord when we pursue rewards. We are not mercenary. They are His gracious idea, expressions of His character and one of His primary motivators to faithfulness. It is *impossible to please Him* apart from such faith. On the other hand, we glorify God when we believe and act on His promised recognition.

Noah: Faith Prepares for the Unseen (7)

(7) We have only promises and descriptions of our kingdom inheritance; we have not seen it. Noah had *not yet seen* rain, but motivated by *reverence* for God and His word, he obediently *prepared* for things to come.

Being convinced of the reality of what he could not see, Noah walked with God and worked for decades on *an ark*. The result? He *became an heir of the righteousness which is according to faith* and inherited a new world after the Flood. If we prepare for it, we too will inherit a new one that we cannot now see.

Faith and the Patriarchs (11:8-22)

Abraham: Faith Waits for the Promises (8-19)

(8-10) When God *called* the father of the faithful from Ur, he *obeyed* to receive his future inheritance just as we must. When *he lived as an alien* in the land all those years, Abraham kept shallow roots *for he was looking for the city which has foundations, whose architect and builder is God*. And when God *tested* him over *Isaac*, he trusted, obeyed and anticipated the promise.

(11-12) *Sarah herself* believed God would keep His promise of a son though it was physically impossible. God continues to reward her faith with *as many descendants AS THE STARS OF HEAVEN IN NUMBER, AND INNUMERABLE AS THE SAND WHICH IS BY THE SEASHORE*. Every Jewish child ever born is part of her reward, an expression of God's faithful, generous heart. Likewise, His rewards to us will far surpass anything that we can imagine.[5]

(13) The author interrupts Abraham's story to stress the kingdom-oriented worldview that drives such faith. *Abraham, Sarah, Isaac, and Jacob* all persisted to the very end *without receiving the promises but having seen them and having welcomed them from a distance, and having confessed that they were strangers and exiles on the earth,* they kept walking and waiting.

Faith walkers envision *the promises* as fulfilled, *welcome* or prepare for their arrival and *confess* or tell others why as they stride forward. This again urges the readers to maintain their walk and witness.

(14-15) *Those who say such things make it clear that they are seeking a country of their own* (Gn 23:4). Their conduct backed up their confession. *And indeed, if they had been thinking of that country from which they went out, they would have had opportunity to return.* They could have retreated, but Abraham and his family did not turn back to what they had left because they knew that what God promised was superior. The drifting Hebrew brothers had the opportunity to return to Judaism. Instead, they could model the fathers and *desire a better country, that is, a heavenly one.*

(16) *Therefore, God is not ashamed* [is pleased] *to be called their God; for He has prepared a city for them.* We who endure will enjoy the same city and country along with God's pleasure with our fidelity.

Scripture tells us enough about the future domain to develop a clear vision of it and what awaits us there. In addition to Hebrews, see for example Psalm 2, 145; Isaiah 2:1-4; 9:1-7; 11; 60-62; 65:17-25 and Revelation 20-22. Shoot mental video clips and replay them again and again to raise your sights.

(17-19) God commanded Abraham to offer Isaac some years after previously promising that *"IN ISAAC YOUR DESCENDANTS SHALL BE CALLED"* (Gn 21:12). How could Abraham reconcile these differing words from God? How could he continue to trust One who seemed to change His mind?

He considered that God is able to raise people even from the dead, from which he also received him back as a type. Faithful obedience is rooted in how one thinks about God. Abraham carefully *considered* what he understood of God's nature. He then minded God's directive, and, in a sense, God did raise Isaac from the dead. After God provided the substitutionary sacrifice, Isaac rose off the altar, prefiguring the resurrection of Jesus.

The repetitive use of *consider* in Hebrews (3:1; 10:24; 11:11, 19; 12:3) is an interesting and powerful admonition. It and the synonym *regard* (10:29; 11:20; 12:5) once again challenge how we think and perceive our world.

Whether or not we understand why God commands us, faith obeys, even amid great confusion and at crushing cost. Abraham did not understand where (8-10), how (11-12), when (13-16) or why (17-19). But he believed, obeyed, and persevered.

Abraham's Sons: Faith Endures unto Death (20-22)

(20-22) The earlier mention of death (13, 19) transitions to the endurance of *Isaac, Jacob,* and *Joseph*. Each walked with God throughout his life, yet none received the promises. Nevertheless, at the end of their lives, they *blessed, worshipped, made mention,* and *gave orders regarding things to come.* They believed that not even death would frustrate the future that God had promised.

The patriarch's certainty that the kingdom promises were true determined where they went (8) and what type of dwellings they chose (9-10). It impacted their marriages (11-12), their child rearing (17-19) and the inheritance they gave them (20-21). Their eternal worldview even affected their burials (22).

Like Abraham, Sarah, Isaac, Jacob, Joseph, and the Hebrews, we are aliens, passing through a foreign, temporary place. We too must act on God's promises of a permanent city (10, 16; 12:22; 13:14) in a particular land (9). It is part of a better, heavenly country (14, 16) in an unshakeable kingdom (12:28).

Faith in the Exodus Era (11:23-31)

Now the writer reveals how faith meets hostility, conflict, and fear which was right where the Hebrews lived.

Moses' Parents: Faith and the State (23)

Based on Moses' beauty and a revelation from God (Ac 7:20),

> Amram and Jochebed regarded God's will concerning the sanctity of life, as more important than obedience to the state, when national law *required* disobeying God's will (cf. Acts 4:19). God honored their faith.[6]

By faith, we must do likewise when called upon.

Moses: Faith Chooses by Eternal Values (24-27)

(24-26) What motivated Moses to choose *ill treatment with the people of God* over the *passing pleasures of sin* available to a prince of Egypt? He valued *the reproach of Christ greater riches than the treasures of Egypt*. Why **choose** rejection and tribulation over earthly power, possessions, and pleasures? *He was looking to the reward.*

Moses weighed out the contrasting principles of earth and eternity and made his history changing resolution. Hebrews who deserted God's people and promises for the passing safety of Judaism were choosing by earth's values and would lose heaven's rewards. Instead, like Moses, *the assurance of things hoped for*—rewards— should be a core value and help frame their decisions. And ours.

(27) From serving in government to fleeing from it, Moses' verdict to follow Christ quickly began to cost him. Realizing his role as the deliverer, *by faith he left Egypt, not fearing the wrath of the king; for he endured, as seeing Him who is unseen.*

God was silent all those years Moses herded sheep in the backside of the desert, but his faith endured. The *conviction of things not seen* kept guiding his steps.

Exodus: Faith Obeys Despite Enemies (28-31)

(28-29) The mention of Pharaoh's wrath suggested *Passover*, the Exodus, and the Egyptian army. Moses and Israel *kept Passover* by obedient faith *so that he who destroyed the firstborn would not touch them* and Israel strode *through the Red Sea* in dry sandals.

Historically, the wilderness travels should fit between verses 29 and 30, but the author omits them because it displays faithless failure to inherit.

(30) Israel's first victory in the fight to possess their inheritance came as they obediently encircled *Jericho*. The Hebrews could take comfort and trust that Christ also oversees their battles and directs them as His household of priests.

(31) *Rahab the harlot* obediently trusted God's character and the promises of His people. Her present risk brought her excellent future reward (Js 6:22-25; Mt 1:4-6) as it will all who do likewise.

Faith After the Exodus (11:32-35a)

After Joshua led Israel into the land God ruled His people through judges and kings. Then He used gentile kings beginning with the Assyrian and Babylonian captivities. Through those tumultuous eras, many of God's faithful ones won magnificent triumphs while others sustained appalling suffering. Well known or anonymous, agony or victory, all believed and persevered in difficult, desperate times and gained heaven's recognition.

(32) Having painted a portrait gallery of enduring faith, the writer asked, *and what more shall I say?* Though their days were the deepest dark, many of the judges such as *Gideon, Barak and Samson* shone as beacons of faith.

(33-35a) Faith overcame or reversed many tests including the *mouths of lions, the power of fire, the edge of the sword*. Some *women* even *received back their dead by resurrection*. Persevering faith remains in all scenarios. Sometimes it delivers from troubles.

Faith from Every Era (11:35b-38)

(35b-37) Despite verses 32-35a above, faith rarely works miracles in our adversities. The distressed readers would have drawn comfort knowing that others with like faith suffered greatly including *mockings, scourgings,* and *imprisonment. Others were tortured, not accepting their release.*

Why refuse the offer of freedom? *So that they might obtain a better resurrection.* These unnamed brothers were convinced of a future resurrection with a special reward that would more than repay their sufferings.

They were stoned while others *were sawn in two.* This is likely a reference to Isaiah. Traditionally, King Manasseh intended to kill him so Isaiah fled and hid within the trunk of a dead cedar tree. The king captured him, left him in it and sawed him asunder.[7]

They went about in sheepskins, in goatskins, being destitute and afflicted while others subsisted in *holes in the ground,* but their faith pressed on.

Such paragons of faith remind us that lack of deliverance or resources does not mean lack of dependence. These heroes *wandered in deserts and mountains and caves and holes in the ground.* A comfortable life and affluence only rarely attended God's models of faith.

Regardless of what confessing faith and prosperity teachers tell us, the norm for faith heroes is suffering and lack. God does indeed promise prosperity but it comes later, in the kingdom, for those who believe and endure.

(38) Indeed, through the writer's quill, God bore witness of them as men and women *of whom the world was not worthy.* He values endurance more than escape. Any Hebrews tempted to flee the faith ought to consider this.

Some Dividends of Faith (11:39-40)

(39-40) All the saints in the chapter *gained* God's *approval through their faith* (11:2, 4-5) but *did not receive what was promised*. God waits to award their inheritance until after the second coming and before the millennium (Dn 12: 2-3, 13; Is 26:19).

Their extraordinary lives of enduring faith are over. Why does God delay their recompense? *Because God had provided something better for us, so that apart from us they would not be made perfect.*

That *something better* is left unexplained, but perhaps it is the opportunity for companionship. Or maybe it refers to the church age, the indwelling Spirit, Jesus our high priest and the house of priests.

We will be involved in some manner when these saints are *made perfect* or receive their inheritance. We will at least watch and celebrate.

Men and women, eminent and insignificant, kings and paupers, princes and prostitutes all walked through life targeting the future kingdom. They waited, decided, served, suffered, withstood severe tests, conquered great enemies, and died, all by faith.

Each of these believers stayed the course and earned God's eternal approval and rewards. The Hebrews are cut of the same cloth and can follow their lead. So are we and so can we.

Positioning for Companionship

1. Share your major take–away from this chapter with your friend.

2. What typically comes to mind when you think "living by faith?" Why do you think that is? What are three decisions you've made that did or may have reflected faith in the opposite world? Talk these over with your companion.

3. As a result of this chapter and our discussion I will;
4. I will start on:

---

[1] Robert N. Wilkin, *The Ten Most Misunderstood Words in the Bible*, Kindle. (Grace Evangelical Society, 2012), 336.

[2] W. F. Moulton and A. S. Geden, *Concordance to the Greek Testament*, Fourth Edition. (Edinburgh: T. and T. Clark, 1963), 810.

[3] My wife coined this phrase to describe the way our family attempts to live.

[4] Thomas L. Constable, "Notes on Hebrews" (2015): 116.

[5] Constable, "Notes on Hebrews," 121.

[7] Emil G. Hirsch et al., "ISAIAH," *JewishEncyclopedia.Com*, n.d., http://www.jewishencyclopedia.com/articles/8235-isaiah.

Chapter 15

Companions Submit to Discipline
(12:1-13)

"I quit!" Do you recall hearing that when you were young, and the game felt unfair or overwhelming to another player? What about the mocking, "Quitter!" when that kid walked away?

The Hebrews are wondering if following Jesus is worth the trouble. Tenacity seems too much to ask after so much suffering, so they're stuffing their hands into their pockets and walking away. Thankfully, the author does not deride them with a snide, "Quitter!" Instead, he encourages them to endure their sufferings as part of their heavenly Father's training for the kingdom.

It can be so very testing to draw near to God when He seemingly fails to deliver us from our problems. Stress, hurt, and confusion unexpectedly smite us, and we cry out to Him, looking for His intervention. But it can feel like He went on vacation with no forwarding address. Surely, you've heard the silence of heaven.

Depending on our situation, support, personality and grasp of God's nature, we may doubt His concern or decide He is untrustworthy. We might become defiant or panic or give up hope and walk away. Or we may believe, submit and endure.

To help his brothers persevere, the author clarifies their view of distresses. He wants them to know that difficulties do not necessarily indicate the Father's displeasure. Instead, He often lovingly employs them as tools to prepare His people for their inheritance just as He did with Israel (Dt 8:1-10). See Appendix 7.

He intertwines athletic (1-4, 12-13) and family (5-11) word pictures to illustrate examples of endurance, the Father's purpose behind their pain and the strength they can draw from one another.

The Examples of Endurance (12:1-4)

An illustration that all the readers would know well, long-distance foot races, prompts them to see themselves as runners who must endure to finish.

Models of Endurance in Suffering (1-2a)

(1a) The *great cloud of witnesses* refers to the saints in chapter 11 who won God's approval, not that they watch us from heaven. As we run our race, their lives testify to us that God notices and rewards those who remain constant and that He wants to affirm our faith one day too (11:2, 4, 39).

(1b) Well aware of his own frailties, the author includes himself in the appeals. Like Greek and Roman athletes who often ran unclothed for freer movement, *let us also lay aside every encumbrance*. We must put off any practice or attitude, even good ones, which impede our pursuit of victory.

The sin that so easily entangles us in Hebrews is departing the faith because of opposition, but any consistent sin trips us up and can sideline us. There are no small sins and no unencumbering sins.

(1c-2a) *Let us run* [Gk. keep on running] *with endurance the* [long distance] *race that is set before us*. The Greek term translated *set before us* seems to indicate that God has marked out or designed each person's race just for him.

One person's course seems mostly uphill and potholed with pain. Meanwhile, another pushes through the dangers on the flatlands of prosperity. Both are unique. Both are tough. Both demand a patient pace and clear focus. Cross-country runners fix their eyes on something ahead, perhaps a tree or a telephone pole, to pull them forward. In the same way, we should keep *fixing our eyes on Jesus.*

The name *Jesus* accents His humanity. A study of the humanity of the Lord as He combatted the aggressive, challenging, Satanic world system can be a tremendous encouragement to our faith.

As the *author* of our faith, Jesus the Man blazed the trail to the kingdom through all challenges. As its *perfecter*, He finished His race to His throne by faith and empowers us with grace, mercy and His intercession to do likewise.

A Motive for Endurance in Suffering (2b-3)

(2b) What prompted Jesus to trust and endure? Reward! *Who for the joy set before Him endured the cross, despising the shame, and has sat down at the right hand of the throne of God.* Foreseeing the endless delight of His future dominion aroused Him to sustain the cross and scorn its dishonor.

(3) If we *consider* [Gk. mediate, mull over] *Him who has endured such hostility by sinners against Himself, we will not grow weary and lose heart.* Focusing on Jesus and the enmity He bore will strengthen us within and steady our stride.

A Measure of Endurance in Suffering (4)

(4) Unlike the Lord, the Hebrews had *not yet resisted to the point of shedding blood in your striving against sin*. The words *not yet* indicate that it was a distinct probability that the readers would suffer more, even to death. *Striving against sin* refers to enduring those sinful men who opposed them as they followed Jesus.

To run with persistence, they must embrace the realities that inheritance demands endurance, suffering is a necessity, even unto death, and Jesus is the perfect model of perseverance.

These verses stress the normalcy of suffering and the fundamental costliness of our inheritance. Neither the Hebrews nor we dare expect a different process. There is no comfortable path to companionship (Ac 14:22).

Expressions of Father's Heart (12:5-11)

The writer now changes pictures to that of the Jewish father rearing his son.

The father was head of the family unit and owner of its property. His word was law and his spiritual and family authority continued until death. Along with love, strength, protection and provision, the father was the primary trainer and disciplinarian of sons.

The future of his sons and family were his focus, especially that of the firstborn. He readied his son to inherit his land and continue his line. Training for the time ahead included spiritual development, verbal instruction and correction, corporal punishment, mental and physical trials, various family responsibilities and learning a trade.[1]

All this, of course, was for the sons and the family's benefit, clear expressions of the father's love. Our heavenly Father has three forward-looking purposes behind His discipline.

Discipline Expresses Love to His Sons (5-6)

(5) Because of their regression and trials, the saints had [Gk. completely] *forgotten the exhortation which is addressed to you as sons* in Proverbs 3:11-12.

> MY SON, DO NOT REGARD LIGHTLY THE DISCIPLINE OF
> THE LORD, NOR FAINT WHEN YOU ARE REPROVED BY

HIM; FOR THOSE WHOM THE LORD LOVES HE DISCIPLINES, AND HE SCOURGES EVERY SON WHOM HE RECEIVES.

The brothers needed to recall that discipline or training is a family affair. *Sons* are not small children. They are those whom the father has publicly recognized (adopted) as adults, legally qualified to inherit (Rm 8:23; Gl 3:23-4:7; Ep 1:5-6). Though eligible for the inheritance they have not yet received it. They could lose it for illicit behaviors such as returning to Judaism, so the good Father disciplines them to ready them for it. What training methods does He lovingly employ?

(5a) He loves by development. As mentioned, discipline looks ahead. In the culture, it referred to training children, sons, athletes, soldiers, orators and even horses for future fitness, all of which included various measures of suffering.

Because He loves us, our Father sends or permits travail to train us for kingdom life. This aspect of His love can be terribly challenging for us to embrace. We popularly view God's love as one that spares pain and gives the good. We can't see how He can hurt us if He loves us. He does love us, and He does hurt us but He will never harm us.

We can also readily embrace a contract mentality, an "if . . . then" view of our relationship with Him. Like the Hebrews, we tend to believe that if we behave, God blesses us. We likely view these blessings as a good life, a worthy family, a measure of success, etc. On the other hand, we quickly assume that severity indicates our sin and God's displeasure.

This is an old covenant perspective. The law promised that righteous actions would produce material blessings while evil actions would curtail them. The new covenant omits such promises for this age. And if this "behavior equals blessing" view is correct, then Jesus was a great sinner. He had the bare minimum of material possessions.

Now, this is not to deny that obedience can bring bountiful temporal blessings. It often does. However, such effects are largely absent for obedient believers outside the Western world. We live in areas where honesty, hard work, goal setting and wise management usually pay off. But it is not necessarily because we obey, for many unbelievers experience the same lifestyles. Instead, under the new covenant, spiritual blessings are the norm (Ep 1:3-14).

Problems and sufferings are part of the growth process and are an ordinary and necessary part of the obedient believer's life (Ac 14:22; Rm 5:1-5; 8:17-39; 2 Cr 1:3-4; 12:7-10; Jm 1:2-12; 1 Pt 1:3-9, et al.). All who aim for godliness will be persecuted (2 Tm 3:12). Peter even describes sufferings *as the true grace of God* (1 Pt 5:6-12). Indeed, almost every passage on trials and suffering in the epistles and Revelation has a positive facet that includes the kingdom in its immediate context.

Thus, suffering is far more preparatory than punitive. It can include punishment, but its primary focus is development. This is to emphasize that we ought not necessarily interpret suffering as proof of sin or indications of God's displeasure.

Love drives all this for THOSE WHOM THE LORD LOVES HE DISCIPLINES. Discipline may include the entire church, *you, your* and *us* (plural) or only the individual believer, *my son* (6x). Either way, the Lord's role as loving father and ours as sons is the heart of the matter.

The Father wants the readers eternal best. As He sees it, the most loving thing for us is to be made like Christ and fit for the kingdom. Inescapably then, both conformity and companionship demand suffering. Thankfully, He may hurt us deeply, but He will never harm us.

(5b) He loves by reproof. Son training includes verbal correction and instruction, for we are not [to] *faint when you are reproved by Him*. He speaks through such means as the Scripture (2 Tm 3:16), authorized teachers (Ti 2:15) and mutual accountability and encouragement (3:12-13). When God reproves us, we must humbly accept it rather than *faint*, that is, quit or withdraw.

(6b) He loves by punishment. THE FATHER ALSO SCOURGES EVERY SON WHOM HE RECEIVES as a companion. No approved son is exempt. In a culture that rebuffs corporal punishment, this statement may offend. We often hear that "God does not punish, he disciplines." However, the text says that he *scourges.*

The Greek term for *scourges* describes Jesus' flogging (Jn 19:1). That horrific beating shredded God's beloved son's neck, shoulders, sides, back, thighs and buttocks, even down to muscle and bone. Why did a loving Father permit Jesus to undergo this? For a greater future purpose—His reign and our salvation.

Our punishment is for past misdeeds, but its tender aim is to break sinful patterns, protect us from self—destructive behaviors and promote self—discipline. Whether by *training*, *reproof* or *punishment*, God is lovingly prepping us to reign with Christ.

Discipline Trains Us to Endure and Inherit (7-8)

(7-8) *It is for discipline that you endure* [Gk. are enduring]. Staying under the gun is training you. *God deals with you as with sons; for what son is there whom his father does not discipline? But if you are without discipline, of which all have become partakers* [Gk. metochoi], *then you are illegitimate children and not sons.* If we will be among the kingdom metochoi, we must be metochoi of discipline.[2] However, we can respond inappropriately.

Illegitimate children are not unbelievers. They are God's children (*you* 2x) who are unable to inherit because they reject His discipline and fall away. They *regard* [it] *lightly* (5a), *faint* (5b), *do not endure* (7-8) and rebel (9) when disciplined. They are still the Father's offspring, but they no longer have the legal right to a kingdom inheritance. "In the Roman world, an 'illegitimate child' had no inheritance rights."[3]

> "Illegitimate" must be understood in its ancient legal sense as descriptive of those who do not enjoy the privileges of the family nor the protection of the father. They are also denied by law the rights of inheritance which belong exclusively to . . . legitimate sons.
>
> Under Jewish law, to be mamzer (to be illegitimate) meant three things: no right of inheritance; no right to marry into Jewish society; and no right to be buried in a Jewish cemetery.
>
> "In the biblical world, a household devoid of discipline was a home where the children had been formally renounced, rejected and disinherited."[4]

Still the father's children, those who reject discipline are not his heirs.

Our attitudes and responses to the discipline of suffering can be eternally unchangeable. Let us choose carefully.

Discipline and Suffering Mature Us (9-11)

Our Father's discipline also works to spiritually mature us.

(9) *We had earthly fathers to discipline us, and we respected them; shall we not much rather be subject to the Father of spirits, and live?* The Father intends that we reverence and submit to Him so that we can *live* physically now to prepare for the kingdom. If we refuse to submit, He may take our life (1 Cr 11:29-32; 1 Jn 5:16-17) ending our training! We lose opportunities here and forfeit rewards there.

(10) Most earthly fathers did the best they could, *for they disciplined us for a short time as seemed best to them* [for this life], whereas our heavenly Father disciplines us perfectly, in light of eternity, *so that we may share His holiness*.

(11) The writer acknowledges the pain, saying that *all discipline*—not some or even most, but all—*for the moment seems not to be joyful, but sorrowful.* Despite the reality of the hurt, just as in athletic training, short—term pain is for long—term gain. *Yet to those who have been trained by it, afterwards it yields the peaceful fruit of righteousness.* Only after the training ends does the fruit of holiness and righteousness issue forth.

The Father's wise discipline affirms His sons, trains them to reign with Christ and matures them.

Strengthen One Another (12:12-13)

Since discipline can be exhausting, the house of priests is to help one another. This is the sixth time the writer exhorts the readers to mutual care (3:12-13; 4:1, 11; 6:10-12; 10:19-25), with more to follow (12:15-17, 25, 28; 13:1-2, 9-17). He gives them two specific responsibilities.

(12-13) Returning to the athletic word pictures, *therefore strengthen the hands that are weak and the knees that are feeble,* so we can serve and walk well together (Is 35:3-4). We can fortify each other spiritually and emotionally when we pray together, listen more than talk, give a hug, read Scripture, just sit and cry together if needed. Few things are more refreshing than genuine fellowship, and few are more debilitating than suffering alone.

Also, *level and straighten* the racetrack of discipleship as much as possible. *Make straight paths* [Gk. running lanes] *for your feet* by removing any hindrances to each other's growth and endurance. Then the *lame* [those limping back to Judaism] *may not be put out of joint*, or dislocated, *but rather be healed* or made functional and persistent again. Since we all partake of discipline, we must all help each other so we can all finish well.

The concerned author reminded his beloved readers that they were in a long-distance race to the kingdom. Pain and suffering attend it, but they had not suffered to the extent Jesus had. They had likewise forgotten the admonition from Proverbs 3:11–12, which teaches that their loving Father uses their anguish to train His sons for their future. For the readers to mature and inherit, they must accept and endure their sufferings and strengthen one another.

Positioning for Companionship

1. Share your major take-away from this chapter.

2. Discuss a period of discipline in your life. Include what God did, how long it lasted, who encouraged you and its various effects.

3. As a result of this chapter and our discussion I will:

4. I will start on:

---

[1] "Family," n.d., https://www.jewishvirtuallibrary.org/family.

[2] J. Paul Tanner, *Hebrews*, ed. Robert N. Wilkin, vol. 2 of *The Grace New Testament Commentary* (Denton, TX: Grace Evangelical Society, 2010), 1088.

[3] Zane C. Hodges, "Hebrews," in *The Bible Knowledge Commentary*, New Testament. (Wheaton: Victor Books, 1983), 820.

[4] Steven Ger, *The Book of Hebrews: Christ Is Greater* (Chattanooga, TN: AMG Publishers, 2009), 209.

Chapter 16

Warning: Obey God's Voice
(12:14-29)

On August 13, 2016, at the Rio Olympics the United States women's rowing 8 extended its undefeated streak to three straight Olympic gold medals and 11th consecutive world title. That level of team dominance is nearly unprecedented at the international level.

The streak is even more impressive when you consider the sport itself. Rowing-specifically the 8, consists of eight rowers and one coxswain-sweep rowing a 62' long boat through the water for 2000 meters (1.24 miles) at speeds around 12 mph. It may have the best claim to being "the ultimate team sport."

Rowing only works if the team works. Winning demands full labor and training, participation, cohesion, and timing of every member to win.[1]

The coxswain is the person who steers the boat and directs team members all through the race. As Katelin Snyder, the coxswain of the US women's eight rowing team told *The Hamilton Spectator* from Rio, she's not just telling the rowers to go faster.

> "'Go faster' could mean pull harder with my arms or it could mean swing more with my body or step quicker with my legs. So when I want them to go faster I have to specify where and how we're going to do that together."[2]

Imagine the feelings of satisfaction, joy, and gratification as the eight stood together on the podium to receive their gold. They worked together and won together.

To finish on the full inheritance medal stand, the priestly house must pull together like an eight-member crew rowing the "big boat" in the Olympics.

How do believer-priests work together to win together? The author weaves the answers to that question into a warning over the danger of unresponsiveness to Christ's word.

We Promote Kingdom Pursuit (12:14-17)

Believer-priests encourage one another to finish strong in two ways.

By Pursuing Relational Health (14)

(14a) Believers are to *pursue* [Gk. as if hunting or chasing] *peace with all men* including those who persecute us. Suffering and serving together can either unite the priestly household or pull it apart.

Our God-given role is to seek the total well–being of the house, including spiritual, emotional, relational and provisional health. When brothers or sisters rupture relations, we are to intervene if they do not work it out within a reasonable time. We can't get along with everyone, but we are to promote peace as much as we can (Mt 5:9; Rm 12:18; 14:19).

(14b) We also pursue together the *sanctification without which no one will see the Lord*. Practical holiness includes a lifestyle devoted to Christ, developed further in the next chapter. *Sanctification* also remains true to Jesus and the fellowship while enduring discipline. Holy relationships help promote healthy relationships.

This team effort readies each of us to *see the Lord. See* is likely a figure of speech that refers to greater personal knowledge of the King. This fellowship occurs now and in the kingdom. Job "saw" or knew and served the Lord more intimately after His travails (Jb 42:5) and *"Blessed are the pure in heart, for they shall see God"* (Mt 5:8).

By Protecting Spiritual Health (15-17)

(15) Each of you *see to it that no one comes short of the grace of God*. The author previously used the phrase *come short* in 4:1 to warn of missing God's *rest*. Here *grace* seems synonymous with the new covenant and its offered companionship. Brothers are to ensure that no one exchanges Jesus and new covenant *grace* for the law and Judaism and so miss their full inheritance.

To passively let others depart can allow a troubling *root of bitterness* to spring up. This allusion to Deuteronomy 29:16-18 describes falling away from the Lord as idolatry that sinks that threatening root among God's people.

> . . . so that there will not be among you a man or woman, or family or tribe, whose heart turns away today from the LORD our God, to go and serve the gods of those nations; that there will not be among you a root bearing poisonous fruit and wormwood.

Roots eventually produce fruit, so if abandonment of Christ weren't eliminated, it would spread among the fellowship and *by it many be defiled*. Sin is addictive and apostasy is contagious, especially under significant pressures. Since the failure of only one individual can affect many others, we must act quickly to protect each other.

(16) Defilement includes brothers becoming *immoral or godless person[s] like Esau, who sold His own birthright for a single meal*. A godless person's values, choices and behaviors are short term and self-serving. *Godless Esau* assessed his *birthright* so lowly that he swapped it evenly, birthright for beans (Gn 25:31-34).

(17) *Even afterwards, when he desired to inherit the blessing, he was rejected*. A blessing was a later legacy after the birthright that the father would pass on to his sons. The elder son received a greater one because he held the birthright. When Esau traded his birthright to Jacob, he lost all legal claim to the firstborn's blessing and ended up with nothing.

He wept over the loss and sincerely regretted what he did, but it was too late *for he found no place for repentance, though he sought for it with tears*. Isaac would not and could not change his mind.

Esau's greater position and privileges as the firstborn came with greater responsibility and, ultimately, greater loss. He fell short of God's grace when he traded away his inheritance for immediate relief from his physical anguish. Still the firstborn son but no longer an heir, his choice was irrevocable.

Likewise, the Hebrew's greater privileges and responsibilities as new covenant priests carried a higher possibility of loss. Should they seek short term physical and emotional comfort in Judaism, they would experience irreversible loss of any further future rewards.

The grace of God offers inheritance; the people of God, both then and now, must promote each other's pursuit of it so that none falls short.

We Hold to the New Covenant (12:18-24)

For leads to reasons why the readers should faithfully cling to their birthright by contrasting the new covenant with the old. Mount Sinai recalls earthly terror associated with the law, whereas Mount Zion summons to future joy in the kingdom.

(18-21) The Hebrew believers *have not come to a mountain that can be touched*. The old covenant fostered chilling, fear-based relationships, for Israel came to *a blazing fire, and to darkness and gloom and whirlwind, and to the blast of a trumpet and the sound of words.*

Such demanding revelation created fear and withdrawal, and the people *begged that no further word be spoken to them*. Even Moses was petrified for *so terrible was the sight that Moses said, "I AM FULL OF FEAR AND TREMBLING."*

(22) In contrast, every new covenant place and person encourages us to hear God and come boldly to Him. *You have come to Mount Zion and to the city of the living God, the heavenly Jerusalem*. Our covenant provides a future heavenly home. It is not an earthly place of *fire and darkness* and fear but the same city that Abraham sought (11:10, 16), the capital city of the eternal kingdom (Rv 21:1-22:5). It is a place of welcome, fellowship, peace and acceptance.

Believers will live in that magnificent capital with *myriads of* [unfallen] *angels,* who serve the King and the saints.

(23) Other inhabitants include *the general assembly* that may refer to a public festival at which all are involved. *The church of the firstborn who are enrolled in heaven.*

> The "church of the firstborn" is evidently another reference to Christ's companions (1:9; 3:12) who are partakers of His glory (3:14; 6:4; 12:8), namely, those who faithfully persevere in their faith.[3]

Recalling them encourages the reader to press on and join them.

The third resident mentioned is *God the Judge of all*. He will judge both their own works for reward and their enemies for retribution. It is an implicit support to press on.

(24) *The spirits of the righteous made perfect* are perhaps Old Testament believers who are *perfect* in spirit but await their resurrection and rewards after the second coming. They may also be all the glorified redeemed, faithful and unfaithful, new covenant and old, whom Christ's sacrifice eventually perfects (10:10, 14; 11:40).[4]

And then there is *Jesus, the mediator of a new covenant, and to the sprinkled blood, which speaks better than the blood of Abel.* Both Abel and Jesus died violently at the hands of their brothers. However, Jesus' blood did not reveal guilt or cry out for justice and retribution as does Abel's (11:4; Gn 4:8-11; Lk 23:33-34).[5] His blood *speaks better* because it mediates the new covenant, providing forgiveness and the grace of a clean conscience.

Why ever consider a return to the thundering, threatening Law? The voice from heaven speaks grace! Let's hear it together.

We Hear and Heed God's Voice (12:25-27)

Now the author spells out the final warning. Like all the previous alerts, the emphasis is on the Hebrews response to the word of God.

The terms *sound of words, heard, begged, words spoken, command* and *speaks* in verses 19, 20 and 24 connect to verses 25-27. *Speaking* in verse 25 is the same term *speaks* in verse 24.

There are three reasons to listen actively to God's voice.

God's Voice Speaks Now in Scripture (25a)

(25a) Israel *begged* not to hear God's voice (19). In contrast, *see to it* [Gk. continuously] *that you do not refuse* [Gk. same term as *begged*] *Him who is speaking* right now in His living, active letter to the Hebrews. Don't cover your ears to the voice of God Himself (1:1-2:5).

God Judges Those Who Reject His Voice (25b)

(25b) An argument of lesser to greater highlights the danger of refusal to hear and obey. *If those* Israelites who *refused* to listen to God when He *warned them on earth did not escape* [lesser], *how much less will we escape who turn away from Him who warns from heaven* [greater]. The question again is, "If God severely judged old covenant apostates what more will He do to those who depart the new covenant?"

The greater accountability rests in the distinctive authority of the mediators and their message. **Moses** spoke **for** God *on earth,* and the **Son** warns **as** God *from heaven.* The present warning, the Book of Hebrews, came from God in *heaven,* and deals with failure to cleave to His Son. The author does not specify the greater judgment because he wants the readers to wonder about the peril.

God's Voice Promises the Kingdom (26-27)

(26) *And His voice shook the earth then* at Sinai. Moving from the shaking of the earth at the giving of the law the writer adapts Haggai 2:6 to speak of two greater shakings: *but now He has promised, saying,* YET ONCE MORE I WILL SHAKE NOT ONLY THE EARTH, BUT ALSO THE HEAVEN. The first is the cosmic shaking and destructions preceding the Second Coming and the millennial kingdom (Hg 2:6-9; Mt 24:29-31; Rv 11:19; 16:17-18).

(27) The second shaking heralds the coming of the eternal kingdom. *This expression,* **"Yet once more,"** *denotes the removing of those things which can be shaken, as of created things, so that those things which cannot be shaken may remain.* The ultimate quaking will replace the millennial earth and cosmos with the eternal kingdom in the new universe.

Only things of eternal value will remain, certainly not Judaism. Heed His reliable, authoritative, final voice. Listen to the Voice from then.

We Operate by Grace (12:28-29)

(28) Now the author applies the warning. *Therefore since we receive* [Gk. are receiving] *a kingdom which cannot be shaken, let us show gratitude. Receive* is present tense because believers **have** already received it by position. We are **now** receiving the kingdom as we endure and prepare for it. We **will** receive it and its rewards when it comes.

Considering such favor *let us show gratitude*. Linguistically, the translation "let us keep on having grace" seems better, for the original term translated *gratitude* is grace.[6] Contextually, we have access to grace that helps (4:16), grace that protects (12:15) and grace that strengthens (13:9). Structurally, grace opened this section (12:15) and now functions as a bookend to close it. The readers will finish strong by new covenant grace. The law offers them nothing with which to worship or serve.

In contrast to the Levites, by grace the Son's priests *may offer to God an acceptable service with reverence and awe*. The Greek term for *service* indicates acts of priestly worship. Offered in *reverence*, deep respect and humility at the King's word animate endurance (5:7; 11:7). *Awe* is a sense of wonder and slight apprehension at God's greatness. Worship prompted by grace is expressed out of a **BIG** view of God. The readers must always recall whom they are privileged to serve.

(29) The writer quotes Deuteronomy 4:24 as a final reason the priestly house must operate and endure by grace: *our God is a consuming fire* who judges **His** people who abandon His covenant for idols.

> *So watch yourselves, that you do not forget the covenant of the Lord your God which He made with you, and make for yourselves a graven image in the form of anything against which the Lord your God has commanded you. For the Lord your God is a consuming fire, a jealous God.*

Should any Hebrew brothers or sisters *forget the* [new] *covenant of the Lord your God* and leave Christ, it would be idolatry. Only fierce temporal judgment from *our God* would remain, perhaps to be experienced in the soon coming Roman destruction of Jerusalem. Those who received such wrath would also forfeit their inheritance as Esau did.

All five warnings have a positive thrust and a negative impetus. God promises present sustaining grace and future inheritance reward to the believer who heeds God's word and draws near Christ's throne.

Enduring obedience under challenging circumstances will result in believers becoming companions with Jesus in His rule. Failure to persevere may result in present discipline similar to what Israel experienced in the wilderness including a forfeiting of inheritance.[7]

God has spoken. Will His people faithfully hear and heed Him?

Positioning for Companionship

1.   Share your major take–away from this chapter with your friend.

2.   Have you ever been a member of a highly productive team? What made it successful? How can you transfer those traits to you and your companion's response to Christ's word as priests caring for one another?

3.   As a result of this chapter and our discussion I will:

4.   I will start on:

---

[1] Louis Bien, "U.S. Women's 8 Is the World's Best Dynasty," SBNation.Com, 13 August 2016, https://www.sbnation.com/2016/8/13/12464972/team-usa-womens-rowing-8-dynasty-rio-olympics-gold-medal.

[2] "What Does a Coxswain in Rowing Do? - Business Insider," n.d., http://www.businessinsider.com/what-does-a-coxswain-in-rowing-do-2016-8.

[3] Zane C. Hodges, "Hebrews," in The Bible Knowledge Commentary, New Testament. (Wheaton: Victor Books, 1983), 811.

[4] Thomas L. Constable, "Notes on Hebrews" (2015): 138.

[5] Constable, "Notes on Hebrews," 138.

[6] A.T. Robertson, Word Pictures in the New Testament (Broadman Press, 1933), 4:442.

[7] Thomas Kem Oberholtzer, "The Warning Passages in Hebrews Part 5: The Failure to Heed His Speaking in Hebrews 12:25-29," BSAC 146.581 (1989): 79.

Chapter 17

Companions Serve His Priestly House
(13:1-19)

A group of retired Marines gathers on Sunday mornings at a local Jack's for biscuits, coffee and Marine solutions to the country's problems. To them it's straightforward: adapt, improvise and overcome. They are friendly, but it's clear that if you're not a Marine, you're not a Marine. They have a special bond forged by Marine history, warrior ethos, core values, tradition and sheer toughness. The Marine Corps motto is *Semper Fidelis*, Latin for "Always Faithful." Their caps, coats and sometimes their lips say, *"Semper Fi!"*

Our King has a special place and role reserved for His followers who are always faithful. They will be companions at His side when He rules the earth. Basic training for companionship includes loyal service in a select corps. That corps is the household of priests.

The author interweaves stern terms such as *prisoners, in prison, ill treatment, afraid, His own blood, suffered* and *bearing His reproach* to remind the readers that the priestly road to partnership is not easy.

As at the end of chapter ten, this passage describes priestly roles companions must fulfill as they train to reign. What are they?

Companion Priests Love (13:1-3)

(1) The summary directive is *let love of the brethren continue*. What does love look like?

Love is Hospitable (2)

(2) Love will *not neglect to show hospitality to strangers*. Teachers, missionaries and fleeing brothers moved homelessly from city to city in the early days to evangelize and equip. Inns were dangerous and unhealthy, so saints often hosted traveling teachers (3 Jn 1:5-8).

Hospitality (Gk. love to strangers) is sharing what you have, where you are, as you are, to aid or encourage another, especially those you don't know or who appear unexpectedly. It is a very concrete expression of love and quite simple if we merely share rather than entertain. Anyone can be hospitable. We all should be (1 Pt 4:9).

Such love may bring a unique blessing *for by this some have entertained angels without knowing it*. Could we be like Abraham (Gn 18), Lot (Gn 19), Gideon (Jg 6), and Manoah (Jg 13) who enjoyed this extraordinary privilege?

Love Remembers the Persecuted (3)

(3) The *prisoners* must have been brothers incarcerated for following Christ. Prisoners under Rome's rule often had to depend on family or friends to provide them with food and other provisions, which the Hebrews could do.

In this way they would *remember the prisoners, as though in prison with them*. To *remember* is to act, not to merely recall. It is to do for an imprisoned brother what we would do for ourselves when possible. It was no easy thing as Paul reveals (2 Tm 1:15-18). Only one family in Asia Minor remembered him when he was imprisoned.

The reason for such love is that *you yourselves also are in the body*, which is a play on words. We are part of the body of Christ that serves and we live in a physical body that feels. We can imagine and empathize with what it would feel like physically, emotionally and spiritually to be *ill-treated* in prison. We also know what we would appreciate brothers doing for us if imprisoned, which may happen in the not too distant future.

Love is an active verb.

Companion Priests Live Morally (13:4-6)
They Practice Sexual Purity (4)
(4) Sex is an amazing gift from God that He wants us to freely enjoy within marriage. His directions for sexual conduct are for our protection and highest pleasure.

Believers must remain sexually pure to *honor marriage* and to keep the *marriage bed undefiled*. The Law directed the Israelites to stone or burn *fornicators and adulterers*. Under the new covenant, *God* [Himself] *will judge* them temporally (1 Th 4:3-8) and such persistent sins undoubtedly cost one his inheritance (1 Cr 6:9-11; Gl 5:19-21; Ep 5:5).

They Develop Contentment (5-6)
(5) Discontentment and greed are major chords in the music of life so *make sure that your character is free from the love of money*. The homeless man under the overpass, the billionaire and everyone in between can love money. It's not a matter of have or have not. It's an issue of the heart, of *character*, the inner man. *To love money* is to desire, pursue and invest it for self. It is the active ambition to find security and pleasure in money and possessions.

> Money is the currency of human resources. So, the heart that loves money is a heart that pins its hopes, and pursues its pleasures, and puts its trust in what human resources can offer.[1]

It is not money itself, but the *love of money*, that is wrong. And it is more than wrong; it is spiritually dangerous (1 Tm 6:6–10, 17-19).

The Hebrew brothers had lost much for following Jesus, including synagogue membership, jobs, property, family and social acceptance. It is easy to see where the drive for possessions and money could arise and be a further temptation to return to Judaism (Jn 16:1-4).

The author's counsel? Be *content with what you have*. Contentment includes living by the truths that we came into the world with nothing, that everything we pursue and cling to will stay here when we depart, and that food and covering are all we truly need for life (1 Tm 6:7-8).

The author acknowledged the struggle between such earthly and eternal principles when he commanded *make sure that your character is free from the love of money*. Contentment is unnatural but it can be learned. Shifting circumstances like those of the Hebrews are core classes in the curriculum (Ph 4:10-14).

One counter to covetousness is giving. Increase or start small but start. Deny yourself one pizza a month this year and ask God who to invest it in. Clean your closets, shop, shed, garage and toy boxes and have a yard sale. Invest the proceeds in the poor. Cut your Christmas budget in half and invest it in a good missionary or Bible college.

The Lord is for us—He has the grace to help us become less covetous and more content. Our part is to **make sure** *that your character is free from the love of money*.

(6) Knowing that fear works against a sense of contentment, the author combines Psalm 118:6 and Deuteronomy 31:6 to remind that

He Himself has said, "I WILL NEVER DESERT YOU, NOR WILL I EVER FORSAKE YOU."

Things always leave us and people sometimes forsake us, but the Savior–King remains. *THE LORD IS MY HELPER, I WILL NOT BE AFRAID. WHAT WILL MAN DO TO ME?* He is here, He is aware and He is able even if our conditions worsen.

Companion Priests Worship (13:7-19)

Church involvement, especially leader–member affairs, has ever been a slow dance between porcupines. Evidently the Hebrews had experienced some leadership changes (7) and some were struggling to obey their current leaders (17), who seem to have scattered throughout the area (24). To help ease the tensions, the author interweaves several directives on corporate life.

Worship Imitates Enduring Past Leaders (7-8)

Second fiddle is the prime position for everyone in the church, for Jesus is the Head and He has appointed various roles to various ones and faithful priests fulfill theirs.

(7) The writer urged the brothers to *remember* and *imitate* their past leaders, centering on their teachings of *the word of God* (Christ and grace) and *the result of their conduct* (a strong finish). The past leaders may have started these house churches. They lived and served with a focus on Christ and grace wrapped in a beautiful balance of life and lip. They spent their lives to the glory of Christ and the good of others This is the target for all present and developing leaders.

(8) Those men were loyal to *Jesus* the man, the ultimate example of endurance. He is also *Christ*, the coming Savior-King, who is *the same yesterday, today and forever.*

The Lord Jesus is undoubtedly immutable, but that is not the meaning here. The author means that just as Jesus was faithful to the Old Testament heroes and the Hebrews previous shepherds, so He would be to the house churches and their new leaders.

Regardless of changing circumstances, Jesus is faithfully consistent with His own. The fellowship is to trust the ultimate Leader and His delegated leaders and follow on.

They Feed on Grace (9-10)
(9) *Believers are not [to] be carried away by varied and strange teachings; for it is good for the heart to be strengthened by grace, not by foods, through which those who were so occupied were not benefited.* Whatever the *strange* teachings were, the saints were responsible for being grounded enough to recognize and reject them.

Perhaps over emphasis on Levitical dietary laws or Essene teachings about food or abstinence attracted some of the Hebrews. Essenes were an ascetic Jewish sect who strongly accentuated foods. They were convinced that the king was on his way, but they did not believe in Jesus as savior or king.

Whoever the delinquent teachers were, the writer once again points the brothers to the teaching of *grace* which strengthens us to endure. As Paul said in Acts 20:32, *"And now I commend you to God and to the word of His grace, which is able to build you up and to give you the inheritance among all those who are sanctified."* It is the teaching of *grace*, not law, that frees and equips believers to inherit.

They Seek Jesus and the Coming City (10-14)
(10) In the sacrificial system, both the priest and the offerors ate of the peace offering to express their fellowship with God (Lv 7:15-17; 30-34). In contrast, *we have an altar* [the sacrifice of Christ and its benefits] *from which those who serve the tabernacle have no right to eat.* Jesus' singular offering rendered obsolete and unacceptable what the Jewish priests offered. Table fellowship is limited to those who believe in Him. To return to the old covenant would be to reject this communion with Christ as our Peace Offering.

(10-12) After God accepted the offerings on the Day of Atonement, *the bodies of those animals whose blood is brought into the holy place by the high priest as an offering for sin, are burned outside the camp.* The high priest burned the unclean remains of the sacrificed bull and goat as part of the closing ceremony. *Therefore, Jesus also, that He might sanctify the people through His own blood, suffered outside the gate.*

Three Gospels record that Jesus was taken "out" to be crucified (Mt 27:32; Mk 15:20; Jn 19:17). His execution *outside the gate* of Jerusalem displayed His rejection by the Jews and symbolized His sanctification of those who follow Him.[2]

(13) Since He suffered for us *outside the gate, let us go out to Him outside the camp.* Our Priest-King was set apart as our sacrifice so that we might be set apart as living sacrifices to Him (Rm 12:1). The Hebrew brothers could leave the old covenant camp of Judaism and be set aside fully to Jesus, *bearing His reproach.* When we publicly identify with Jesus, we will suffer similar effects, such as rejection, injustice, cursing, beating, and even death.[3]

(14) To leave the camp was a wise thing, *for here we do not have a lasting city, but we are seeking the city which is to come.* Earthly Jerusalem was no longer the capital of the Hebrews' homeland, nor would it last much longer (Lk 19:41-44; 21:20-24). Heavenly Jerusalem was now their home, and they must move toward it.

They Offer Spiritual Sacrifices by Grace (15-19)

Leaving the Temple and its system doesn't do away with sacrifices. Instead, *through Him then* we royal priests present different types of offerings.

(15) The sacrifice of witness. *Let us continually offer up a sacrifice of praise to God,* explained as *the fruit of lips that give thanks to His name.* The Greek reads "the fruit of the lips that confess His name," as in baptism, conversation and witness.

The author again reiterates "continue your confession." They certainly struggled with maintaining both their original and ongoing affirmation of Jesus (3:1; 4:14; 10:23; 11:13; 13:6). To view witness as worship may help them do so. Perhaps if we saw evangelism as *a sacrifice of praise,* we would offer it up more gladly, more often.

(16) The sacrifice of good works and giving. *And do not neglect doing good and sharing, for with such sacrifices God is pleased.* Service in the fellowship and the community please God as worthy priestly service (Mt 5:16; Ac 9:36-43). Giving is a priestly offering when done with the right motives (2 Cr 9:12-15; Ph 4:18).

One could only make offerings at specific times under the old covenant. Under the new, we confess Christ, do good works and share *continually.* Worship is our way of life (Rm 12; Jm 1:26-27; 1 Pt 2:4-10).

(17) The sacrifice of obedience to spiritual leaders.

The idea of submitting to an elder or pastor is foreign to many American believers. They move from assembly to assembly and take or leave spiritual directions as if they are tweets. No one is going to tell them what to do. Yet the God of the Word says, *obey your leaders and submit to them*. God established and expects the church to work within hierarchical leadership.

The Trinity best models the command and pattern of *obey your leaders and submit to them*. Father, Son and Spirit are equal persons but have different roles. Though equal, Son and Spirit submit to the Father and the Spirit to both Father and Son. This is God's model of leadership and followership for marriage and the church: equality in person but difference in position and function (Gn 1:26-28; 2:18-25; 1 Cr 11:1-12; Ep 5:22-33; 1 Pt 5:1-5).

It takes much love and humility to lead well or to follow well. God calls church leaders to model integrity and faithfulness. They are to teach grace and direct by lowly service, and practical love with spiritual and relational care.

Followers are to submit humbly and serve as faithful, active priests. The Lord intends to raise the younger ones to leadership in His time, so He encourages them to submit to the older as training. The best leaders are first good followers (1 Pt 5:1-7).

> "The leaders [elders or pastors] keep watch over [our] souls, and will have to give an account to God, one day, for their stewardship over us. We should make their work in this life easier for them, by being obedient and submissive to them."[4]

(18) The sacrifice of intercession. Finally, keep on *praying for us* — the author and the brothers with him. Had the author's plans been called into question or had he been accused of something? Perhaps he was among the departed leaders and his absence was misunderstood. We cannot know, but the comment *for we are sure that we have a good conscience, desiring to conduct ourselves honorably in all things* seems to indicate something was amiss. He wanted their prayers because he aimed to keep his behavior pure.

(19) *I urge you all the more to do this, so that I may be restored to you the sooner.* He knew and missed them (the readers knew who wrote Hebrews!) and wanted to join his friends once again. Face-to-face care is always better than phone calls, letters, emails, texts or Facebook, as helpful as they are.

The corporate priesthood of believers is an overlooked and much needed truth in our Westernized church. Ministry is not for select professionals; it is for all believer-priests.

This section strongly reminds us that specific, consistent function in what we call "our church" is central to the life of an emerging companion. It appears to be a rarity in the average American fellowship.

> 20% of the people volunteer for 80% of the ministries and contribute 80% of the budget to the church. Conversely, 80% of the church body does only 20% of the ministry and 20% of the giving.[5]

We have much opportunity to improve as a household of priests both within and without our church buildings. We priests who enduringly love the fellowship, live morally and worship acceptably will ultimately become Christ's companions. Semper Fi!

Positioning for Companionship

1. Share your major take—away from this chapter with your fellow priest.

2. Evaluate your consistent priestly service. Which is strongest: loving the fellowship, living morally or worshipping acceptably? How do you know? The weakest? Share these with your companion and make a simple plan together to strengthen the weak one.

3. As a result of this chapter and our discussion I will:

4. I will start on:

---

[1] "What It Means to Love Money," Desiring God, 26 July 2012, https://www.desiringgod.org/articles/what-it-means-to-love-money.
[2] Thomas L. Constable, "Notes on Hebrews" (2015): 145.
[3] Constable, 145.
[4] Constable, 146.
[5] Bill Fredric Korver, "Biblical Uses of Reward as a Motivation for Christian Service" (D.Min., Liberty University, 2011), 3.

Chapter 18

Companions Rely on the Great Shepherd
(13:20-25)

If you were learning to fly, you'd quickly discover that taking off on a calm day is close to a piece of cake. Get a Cessna 150 to speed and it rises off the runway almost on its own, with just a slight pull of the yoke. On the other hand, landing can be the biggest challenge of your sky–high experience. Ask any pilot.

Putting a sermon on the ground and shutting off the engine can be trying too. Ask any preacher (or maybe a listener!). But the author of Hebrews had no trouble. He concludes his encouraging written sermon with a prayerful blessing and some personal information.

You can feel the author's affection and heart for the readers as he dips his pen in the ink one last time and scratches the blessing across the parchment. It is somewhat reminiscent of Numbers 6:22-27 and focuses on God's provision and purpose for believers through Jesus.

He bundles several of the primary themes of Hebrews and adds some new ones. Together, they exalt the Lord Jesus Christ and remind the readers that He is all they need and they desperately need Him. This doxology is a beautiful way to finish what he had to say.[1]

A Prayerful Blessing (13:20-21)
Based on God's Provision in Jesus (20)
(20) The author calls on *the God of peace* for that is what He provides. The Hebrew concept of *peace*—shalom—includes both the absence of conflict and the presence of fullness, satisfaction or happy contentment. It's the idea of life as God originally intended in Eden, a well-rounded, prosperous, fulfilling life of dependency. Life in the future kingdom that we can foretaste today.

Peace grants emotional rest amid relational and circumstantial troubles. Demanding, difficult days cry out for *peace*. Until we live in the land of shalom, let's recall that real *peace* now rests only in God.

The God who grants peace *brought up from the dead the great Shepherd of the sheep,* the first explicit mention of Jesus' resurrection in the book. Resurrection made Him our *great* [incomparable] *Shepherd. Shepherd* is an Old Testament title often used to describe kings and of course, those who herd sheep. Both types of shepherd's care and provide for their flock and are sovereign over it. It is a reminder that sheep cannot survive without their shepherd and that we have an unmatched *great Shepherd* (Is 63:11).

Christ's resurrection came *through the blood of the eternal* [new] *covenant* in contrast to the temporary old one enacted with inferior animal blood. His crucifixion mediated it and His resurrection and ascension made Him the High Priest who applies it today. The new covenant will also be the basis for the initiation of His kingdom (Ek 37:26; Mt 26:28-29). Thus, He is now Son-Priest-King, *Jesus our Lord.*

Jesus is not only the Great Shepherd, He is the Good Shepherd (Jn 10:14), the Chief Shepherd (1 Pt 5:4) and My Shepherd (Ps 23:1). [2] Warren Wiersbe said it so well:

> As the Good Shepherd, Jesus Christ died for the sheep (Jn 10:11). As the Great Shepherd, He lives for the sheep in heaven today, working on their behalf. As the Chief Shepherd, He will come for the sheep at His return (1 Pt 5:4). Our Shepherd cares for His own in the past, present, and future. He is the same yesterday, today, and forever![3]

Thus, the benediction begins with an appeal to what God freely provides in Jesus. He brings peace amid conflict. He is the living, ruling, caring, leading, great new covenant Shepherd. Should martyrdom be called for, He is the source of resurrection. He indeed is *Jesus our Lord*.

For God's Purpose Through Jesus Christ (21)

(21) God intends that *Jesus our Lord equip you in every good thing*. Fishermen fit or mend their nets to make them useful and productive (Mt 4:21). In the same way Christ repairs and readies us *to do His will*, to live to inherit the kingdom. God is *working in us that which is pleasing in His sight* with many tools, including ongoing trials, and all are *through Jesus Christ*.

> Now that He is in heaven, He is working *in* us, to mature us in His will and bring us to a place of spiritual perfection.[4]

The writer's burden was that his readers submit to God's will of suffering and remain dedicated to Jesus so they will inherit companionship. Such a finish will resound to His *glory forever and ever. Amen.*

Some Personal Information (13:22-25)

(22) The author makes his final core appeal: *Bear with* [listen carefully and apply] *this word of exhortation, for I have written to you* *briefly*. This book of encouragement really is brief. It takes less than an hour to read aloud. Yet how many times has he urged them to hear and heed the Word? Over thirty!

(23) The author planned to visit shortly, hopefully with Timothy alongside. *Take notice that our brother Timothy has been released, with whom, if he comes soon, I will see you.* This is the only reference in Scripture to *Timothy* as a prisoner, who faithfully endured his trial. He took Paul's admonition to heart (2 Tm 1:8).

(24) The author instructed them to *greet all of your leaders and all the saints*. The third mention of the *leaders* in the chapter, there must have been a few issues within the fellowship. To *greet* them all would connect the church *leaders* and the members and encourage all the priestly house, even those slipping back to the Temple.

Those from Italy [who] *greet you* may have resided in Italy or were among those once expelled from Rome and now scattered through the empire (Ac 18:2).

(25) The final benediction *grace be with you all* reminds again that new covenant grace, not law, would strengthen them to persevere (2:9; 4:16; 10:19; 12:15; 13:9).

If Hebrews went to saints in or near Jerusalem, it seems to have worked. Eusebius, an early church historian (c. 260-339), and bishop of Caesarea tells us that the Jerusalem believers escaped the Roman destruction.

> But the people of the church in Jerusalem had been commanded by a revelation, vouchsafed to approved men there before the war, to leave the city and to dwell in a certain town of Perea called Pella. And when those that believed in Christ had come thither from Jerusalem, then, as if the royal city of the Jews and the whole land of Judea were entirely destitute of holy men, the judgment of God at length overtook those who had committed such outrages against Christ and his apostles, and totally destroyed that generation of impious men.[5]

As our culture quickly turns against us, may we be like the Hebrews. Men and women, boys and girls of faith who heed the Son's word, draw near His high priestly throne, persevere our trials and seek His rewards. Let us become the King's companions.

Positioning for Companionship

1.   Share your major take-away from this chapter with your fellow priest.

2.   Discuss your major take-away from Hebrews with him or her.

3.   As a result of Hebrews and our conversation I will:

4.   I will start on:

---

[1] Morris, Leon, *Hebrews*, vol. 12 of *The Expositor's Bible Commentary* (Grand Rapids: Zondervan, 1981), 154.

[2] Thomas L. Constable, "Notes on Hebrews" (2015): 146.

[3] Warren W. Wiersbe, *Be Confident* (Colorado Springs, CO: David C. Cook, 1982), 155.

[4] Wiersbe, *Be Confident*, 155.

[5] *Eusebius: Church History, Life of Constantine the Great, and Oration in Praise of Constantine*, vol. 1 of *A Select Library of the Nicene and Post-Nicene Fathers of the Christian Church, Second Series* (Christian Literature Company, 1890), 138.

Appendices

Appendix 1

Salvation

When the curtain closed on Day Six of creation week, *God saw all that He had made, and behold, it was very good*. The first couple was literally in paradise on earth. Their new life consisted of perfect fellowship with God and one another, obeying His one rule and reigning over the earth. They reveled in God's intent for man, eternal life on earth.

But you know the story. The serpent staged a coup d'état and God's servant–king joined him. Adam's transgression shattered communion, twisted obedience into rebellion and gave away dominion (Lk 4:5-7).

But God stepped in. He promised to defeat the devil and save.

The Meaning of Salvation

When we hear "save" or "salvation," we tend to instinctively think of delivery from eternal condemnation to eternal life. This indeed occurs when a person trusts Jesus, but that is not the primary meaning or use of salvation.

At its most basic, salvation is deliverance from one state to another. That change of status might be from any number of things such as from danger to safety (Ex 14:30; Mt 14:30), troubles to tranquility (Pr 34:6; Mt 14:30-32), or from illness to health (Ps 103:3; Mt 9:22). It liberates from enemies to security (Ps 18:3; Lk 1:71), from God's temporal wrath to peace (Jo 3:7-10; Rm 5:5-11) and from spiritual death to spiritual life (Ek 36:22-38; Ep 2:1-10). Temporal rescue is the primary way the Bible uses salvation.

Thus, salvation includes both the physical and the spiritual, the temporal and eternal. It is this broad nature of salvation that we often overlook.

The Purpose of Salvation

Salvation is part of God's larger purpose.

At the dinner party at Zacchaeus' home Jesus said, *"for the Son of Man came to seek and to save that which was lost."*

Note His terms. He is the *Son of Man*, the human-divine Savior-King. His mission? *To seek and to save **that** which was lost*. "That" is a neuter relative pronoun. It refers to more than people.

What was lost? Paradise on earth: God's earthly kingdom in a perfect universe ruled with His people in unbroken fellowship and followership.

Jesus came to do what God promised in Eden. He would send the Warrior-Rescuer to fight the rebel (*I will put enmity between your seed and her seed*), defeat him and his rebellion (*He shall crush you on the head*), and restore God's earthly kingdom by death and resurrection (*you shall bruise him on the heel*).

> *The Son of God appeared for this purpose: to destroy the works of the devil.* (1 Jn 3:8)

Satan knows very well that this is God's resolve. That is why he tempted Jesus with a cross-free kingdom if He would only acknowledge his authority and worship him once (Lk 4:5-8). He tried the same offer a couple of years later through Peter (Mt 16:21-23) and again at Golgotha (Mt 27:41-42; Mk 15:32; Lk 23:35-37).

According to Revelation 5, the last battle in the war draws near. Christ, the Lion and the Lamb, the Warrior-Rescuer, has come, died and risen (6-9a). In this He redeemed people (9b), regained the right to rule (9, 12–13), and renewed believers' right to rule (10).

In the future (Rv 20-22), Jesus will complete the serpent's defeat (20:1-2, 10), remake creation (20:11; 21:1) and assume His earthly throne. Unlike Eden, this time man will forever fellowship (22:3a, 4, 5a), follow (3b) and rule (5b) on a new earth in a new heaven. *The Son of Man* will have saved *that which was lost* and restored His realm, His rule and His co-rulers.

Therefore, the ultimate purpose of salvation is to restore His earthly kingdom ruled by man. This will glorify God by vindicating His sovereignty. The secondary intent is to benefit us.

The Types of Salvation

Four rescues must occur to restore God's reign.

Universal Salvation

The cross cleansed and positionally reconciled all things—the heavens, the earth and man (Co 1:15-20; Hb 9:22-24). He will begin to progressively renew the heavens and earth during the Millennium and ultimately replace them during the Great White Throne (Ac 3:19-21; Rv 20:11; 21:1).

The restored kingdom will be centered upon the new earth in a new heaven, just as in Eden. The spiritual and physical salvation of the universe will deliver from the curse of sin into glorious freedom (Rm 8:18-25). It will restore the perfect physical realm of God's kingdom.

National Salvation

God will one day make Israel His treasured, holy, priestly nation as He intended (Ex 19:1-6), but they must first be born again (Ek 36:22-38; Jn 3:7). This will occur as the Jewish remnant watches Christ return at the end of the Tribulation and believes in Him (Zc 12:10-13:1; 13:9-14:9; Rm 11:25-32).

Their deliverance will include spiritual rebirth, release from Tribulation wrath and victory over all enemies. Israel will then be the head nation under Christ forever. Israel's rescue will provide the spiritual, political and commercial capital of the kingdom just as Eden did initially (Is 60).

The Lord will also redeem many nations who will enjoy the kingdom (Ps 2:6; Zc 2:10-11; 14:16; Rv 21:22-27). The salvation of the nations will reverse the judgment of Babel and fill the earth with God's Gentile people.

Thus, national salvation will place Israel and the nations in the kingdom.

Church Salvation

We trust Jesus individually. Just as no one can eat for us, no one can believe for us. That rests with us alone. But when we believe, we are made part of an eternal community that plays a central kingdom role in our lives now and forever.

God is a communal person, a Trinity, and the Bible is a corporate book. Its viewpoints are **we**-oriented rather than **me**-centered. Middle Eastern people were and are much more concerned with family, tribal and national image than self-image.

Israel the nation consists of twelve tribes. The priesthood is from the tribe of Levi. One family therein, Aaron's, provided the high priests. David and Jesus come from Judah, the tribe of kings. It's all about belonging to a group through which God works.

The New Testament follows suit. It presents the church in collective word pictures. A *temple* consists of many *stones*. A *body* has many *members*. Multiple *priests* comprise a *household*. A single *flock* has many *sheep*.

These corporate metaphors remind us that we are part of something much more extensive than ourselves. Our salvation is about our life as part of the universal and local church, Christ's greater group.

We became part of His espoused bride when we believed in Jesus. The first Adam had a pure bride to help him rule the earth, and so will the last Adam (2 Cr 11:2; Rv 19:7-8). Jesus is now sanctifying His church to make her His holy, beautiful bride who will share His rule (Ep 5:25-27).

The great Husband bought His bride, sanctifies her, anticipates their wedding. He will celebrate her at a great feast and share His eternal glory with her.

Church salvation provides a beautiful queen to co-rule the kingdom with Christ. At this point the Jews, the Gentiles and the Church will be established in the kingdom with their various roles.

And of course, saved individuals make up these groups.

Individual Salvation

Our salvation begins when we believe in Jesus. At that instant God gives us eternal life and we possess it forever.

What is eternal life? Most assume that it means to live forever. It does, but that is an insufficient definition, for all men live forever, even unbelievers.

Saved persons live with God's kind of life, an endless quality of life that begins now. Jesus described it as a relational knowledge of the Father and Himself (Jn 17:3).

> *This is eternal life, that they may know You, the only true God, and Jesus Christ whom You have sent.*

It is not knowing about God, it is knowing Him. All believers have this, even the disloyal. However, the Greek indicates that we may or may not develop this indescribable relationship. We either pursue Christ and eternal life as our lifestyle now or we relegate them to the afterlife. That decision affects us now and in the kingdom.

Note how eternal life relates to the kingdom.

Regeneration eternal life: Eternal life begins with spiritual birth or regeneration. Jesus revealed the necessity and some benefits of it in John 3.

We need it because we can neither see nor enter the kingdom (3:3, 5) without it. We have no spiritual life (3:5-8) and are perishing now, already condemned (3:16-18). Thankfully, regeneration provides everything we lack.

Eternal life includes kingdom citizenship (3:3, 5) a God–like spiritual nature with the capacity to grow (3:6-8; 4:13-14), deliverance from condemnation (3:16-18) and many other blessings such as righteousness and forgiveness.

Regeneration is the foundation for life in the kingdom. We receive kingdom entrance (Jn 3:3, 5), adoption as sons who possess the right to inheritance (Gl 3:23-4:7), the Holy Spirit for righteous living (Gl 5:16-26) and of course, opportunity and ability to earn rewards. (Ep 2:8-10).

How do we receive new birth? By belief in Jesus (3:15-18, 36). Eternal life is a gift received by grace alone through faith alone in Jesus alone. It begins now rather than when we enter heaven.

Sanctification eternal life: If regeneration is the foundation of kingdom life, then sanctification is the preparation for it. Don't confuse the two. In the first, we believe in Jesus. In the second we behave as He instructs. The first is purely a gift. The latter demands our works. The first gives us kingdom entrance. In the second we work for kingdom rewards.

You can usually tell when sanctification life is under discussion in the text. It will be an encouragement or statement of present motives or responsibilities. It is often also combined as a current activity considering future eternal life (Jn 12:24-26; 1 Cr 9:24-27; Gl 6:6-10; 1 Tm 6:17-19; 2 Tm 4:6-8). These texts often use the term or idea of rewards.

In sanctification life we train to reign in the kingdom. The quality of our preparation will determine our kingdom status and roles, our destiny there. Sanctification or growth is not automatic nor is it universal. Some believers fail to pursue spiritual growth and waste their time of preparation. All believers will live in the kingdom but only the steadfast will gain high position and reward.

Kingdom position is where self–denial, submission, service, sacrifice and suffering come in. Believers who live this way will enjoy an abundant eternal life both now and forever (Mt 16:24-27; 19:27-30; Gl 6:6-10; Co 3:22-25).

That is what Jesus did and as with Him, it will issue in a more lavish kingdom experience for us (Mt 16:21-23; Hb 12:2). The Father will honor and reward those who pursue Jesus in this way (Mt 16:27; Jn 12:26).

Honor and reward will include victors' crowns, eternal treasures, perhaps ruling a nation or a city, special companionship with Jesus or a secret name known only by you and Him (Mt 6:19-21; Lk 14:12-15; 1 Cr 9:24-27; Gl 6:7-9; Co 3:22-25; 2 Tm 2:12; Rv 2-3). There are many others.[1]

Believers who fall away from Jesus or waste life grabbing for present gusto will forever lose many or all these privileges.

Picture your relationship with God as a lightbulb, the brighter the better. Fellowship and faithfulness determine your intensity now and forever. You die today and enter eternity shining at 1600 lumens. You will continue to grow and serve from the 1600 level forever. Your friend arrives there at 450 lumens. He will ever be 1150 lumens behind you. There will be no comparison or sorrow, jealousy or shame, but there will be eternal distinctions in roles and responsibilities. Today is our only time to prepare our kingdom status (1 Tm 6:12).

Glorification eternal life: Regeneration gave us a kingdom destination with eternal dynamic and duration of life. Sanctification prepares our kingdom destiny. In glorification we will ever delight in our kingdom destiny and roles. It includes two phases.

Phase one of glorification life begins at the Rapture and is entirely by grace. God will give us our resurrection bodies. Our sin nature and mortal bodies will be gone. He will fully conform us to Christ and fully restore His image. We will be physically, mentally, socially and spiritually ready for kingdom life (Rm 8:30).

Phase two is by reward for works and occurs at the judgment seat (1 Cr 3:15; 9:27; 2 Cr 5:10; Rv 22:12). Following receipt of our resurrection body, the Lord will evaluate the quality of our Christian works, our sanctification life. The ensuing gain or loss of reward, our kingdom status, is also referred to as eternal life or life in the kingdom (Mt 19:29; 25:46; 1 Tm 6:12; Jd 1:21, etc.). See table page 198.

The Results of Salvation

Salvation will rescue, restore and renew God's earthly kingdom. Note the connection between the original and eternal realms.

> *Then God said, "Let Us make man in Our image, according to Our likeness; and let them rule over the fish of the sea and over the birds of the sky and over the cattle and over all the earth, and over every creeping thing that creeps on the earth." God created man in His own image, in the image of God He created him; male and female He created them. God blessed them; and God said to them, "Be fruitful and multiply, and fill the earth, and subdue it; and rule over the fish of the sea and over the birds of*

> *the sky and over every living thing that moves on the earth."*

God's image includes fellowship. He is a Triunity [*Us*], who fellowships with Himself, so He made mankind to relate with Him and each other. God operates in a hierarchy of authority. Scripture reveals that all three persons fulfilled different roles in creation. In all their work, the Son submits to the Father and the Spirit to the Father and Son. Thus, man is made to follow God's word. Finally, God is the eternal king who created us to rule the earth. So, the image of God includes our roles of **fellowship**, **followership** and **rulership**.

Note a summary of our lives on the new eternal earth (Rv 22:3-5).

> *There will no longer be any curse; and the throne of God and of the Lamb will be in it, and* **His bond-servants will serve Him** [followership]; **they will see His face, and His name will be on their foreheads** [fellowship]. *And there will no longer be any night; and they will not have need of the light of a lamp nor the light of the sun, because the Lord God will illumine them and* **they will reign forever and ever** [rulership].

As formerly mentioned, the ultimate purpose of salvation is to restore the kingdom and glorify God by vindicating His sovereignty. Paul summarizes this in 1 Corinthians 15:20-28.

> *But now Christ has been raised from the dead, the first fruits of those who are asleep. For since by a man came death, by a man also came the resurrection of the dead. For as in Adam all die, so also in Christ all will be made alive. But each in his own order: Christ the first fruits, after that those who are Christ's at His coming, then comes the end, when He hands over the kingdom to the God and Father, when He has abolished all rule and all authority and power. For He must reign until He has put all His enemies under His feet. The last enemy that will be*

abolished is death. For He has put all things in subjection under His feet. But when He says, "All things are put in subjection," it is evident that He is excepted who put all things in subjection to Him. When all things are subjected to Him, then the Son Himself also will be subjected to the One who subjected all things to Him, so that God may be all in all.

That is salvation. It is for God's glory and our good and it all centers on the kingdom.

Regeneration Eternal Life	**Sanctification Eternal Life**	**Glorification Eternal Life**
Reception of eternal life	Application of eternal life	Recognition of eternal life
Kingdom entrance	Kingdom training	Kingdom status and role
Fellowship begins	Fellowship grows	Fellowship grows
A gift	A result	A gift and a reward
By grace through faith	By faith working through love	By grace and works
Determined at belief	Determined in lifestyle	Determined at the Bema
Our kingdom destination	Our kingdom development	Our kingdom destiny
Actual	**Possible**	**Actual**

It should be clear now that we must pay close attention to a passage when we see the term salvation, eternal life or cognates. To automatically read it as "go to heaven" can create many problems. It will twist the meaning of the text. Devastating thoughts such as, "Can I lose my salvation?" or "I'm not sure I'm saved!" can occur.

It can also distort our view of God and His grace, and our understanding of heaven, rewards and good works.

There are many salvation terms in Scripture including redeem, redemption, save, heal, reconcile, and deliver. When you see one of these in your Bible reading, learn to ask: does this context refer to temporal or spiritual deliverance? If spiritual, is it universal, national, church or individual? And if personal, does it speak of regeneration, sanctification or glorification?

Finally, after all this information, most important of all, do you possess eternal life?

The declaration of the Bible is to believe in Jesus for eternal life. He can provide it because He is God who died to pay for your sins and provide the righteousness that God demands and you lack. Jesus rose from the dead to declare unmistakably that He is the Son of God and that He did all that God requires of you. Jesus is therefore able to give you eternal life.

That is what Jesus did. Eternal life is what He promises. Your role is to believe in Him. To believe is to be convinced or persuaded that His promise is true for you.

Do you believe this?

---

[1] Bob Wilkin, "Hating Your Life to Keep It for Eternal Life John 12:25," *Grace in Focus*, n.d., https://faithalone.org/magazine/y2005/05_78_1.html.

Appendix 2

The Kingdom

What is the kingdom? What do we mean when we talk about it as the place of reward, companionship and our eternal home? Let's summarize it.

What "Kingdom" Means

There are three primary forms of God's kingdom. First is the **eternal, universal kingdom** over which He has always ruled everything (1 Tm 1:17).

Then came the **original earthly kingdom** in Eden (Gn 1:26-28). Life there was to be the eternal enjoyment of fellowship, followership and rulership. It was paradise on a new earth in a new universe for God's and man's pleasure. It was a theocracy, that is, God's indirect rule on earth through a human mediator.

When Adam rebelled, sin and death entered, and he gave his rule to Satan who has controlled the world ever since (Lk 4:6; Jn 12:31; 1 Jn 5:19).

We can call the second form is what this author calls **the national kingdom**. God ruled the nations through government and His people through Noah, Abraham, and on through Moses, Joshua, the judges, kings and prophets until Jesus came. He promised a global domain, with a special national role for Israel.

Israel rejected Jesus as Savior–King so the kingdom is delayed. The church is not the kingdom. The church prepares people for the kingdom. We preach the gospel of eternal life that grants kingdom entrance to those who believe in Jesus. We also disciple believers which prepares them for the kingdom. We are to do this in all nations until the King returns to rule (Ac 1:6; 14:22; 1 Cr 4:8; 2 Tm 4:1; 2 Pt 1:11; 3:1-3; Rv 5:9-10; 20:4).

The last domain will be His **restored eternal earthly kingdom** (Dn 2:44; 7:13-14, 27; Rv 21:1-22:5). The Bible refers to it as *the kingdom of heaven, the kingdom of God, David's kingdom, My kingdom* and *the kingdom of the Son of his love,* among others, depending on context.

Kingdom reestablishment will occur in two phases.

Phase 1: The Millennium
What the Millennium Is
Millennium is Latin for "1000 years" (Rv 20:1-7) when King Jesus and some saints will rule on the earth (Is 2:1-2). It is step one in full recovery of God's sovereignty and will begin shortly after the Second Coming.

Inhabitants of the Millennium
No unbelievers will live in the kingdom when it starts and Satan will be locked away until the end, while resurrected saints from all ages will be there (Dn 12:2, 13; Rv 1:6; 2:26-27).

It will be home for all Jewish and Gentile believers who survive the Tribulation along with the children they will have during the

Millennium (Mt 26:31-46; Zp 3:20). All Jewish children will believe in Jesus while many of the Gentile offspring will not (Zc 14:17-19).

Of course, angels and nations will also be present.

Spiritual Life in the Millennium
Universal worship will center in the temple in Jerusalem (Zc 14:16-21; Ml 1:11). Righteousness, peace, joy and knowledge of the Lord will be the norm (Is 11:6-9; Hb 1:8; Rv 2:27).

There will be many unbelievers but outright personal and national sin will be severely judged (Ps 2:10-12).

Physical Life in the Millennium
We will live in our glorified bodies like that of Jesus, free of any hindrance.

Non—resurrected life spans will be quite extended, as in the pre—flood world (Is 65:20). Illness, disease, deformity and death will be sporadic (Is 34:24; 35:5-6). All will be healthy, well off, free to develop their skills and talents, and enjoy their work. All of life will be fulfilling.

As for the earth, the times of global rebirth (Mt 19:28), refreshing (Ac 3:20) and restoration (Ac 3:21) will begin. Christ will lessen the curse on creation and partially renew the earth (Is 32:13-15; Rm 8:19-23). Crops will be incredibly productive (Is 30:23-26; Am 9:13) and animal life will be as it was before the fall (Is 65:25).

Government and National Life in the Millennium
The Lord Jesus Christ will be the universal King (Ps 2; Zc 14:9) and Jerusalem will be the world capital (Is 2:1-4).

Resurrected David will be His vice-regent, the prince of Israel (Jr 30:9; Hs 3:5). Israel will be the lead nation (Dt 15:6; 28:13; Zc 8).

Many saints will share Christ's rule over cities, regions, etc. Some will rule the nations with a rod of iron (Rv 2:26-28). We will help make legal judgments for people and angels (1 Cr 6:1-3).

Scripture mentions Egypt, Iran, Iraq and Syria, north and middle Jordan, Sinai, Saudi Arabia, the Gaza strip, Lebanon. There will be many others (Dn 7:13-14). Each will have a king who will serve under Israel and Church age saints.

Economic Life in the Millennium

Everyone will work, including us (Is 65:21, 23; Ek 34:26). There will never be poverty, unemployment or depressions unless Christ disciplines a nation. The nations will typically be wealthy and bring it to Israel. It seems that agriculture and trade will be primary parts of the global economy (Is 60:4-8).

The End of the Millennium

At the close of the Millennium, Jesus will release the devil who will lead one last global rebellion against Christ and his people (Rv 20:7-10). All who did not believe in Jesus as Savior—King during the Millennium will follow him. They will resent His rule and the devil convince them to follow his rule and overthrow Christ. This will show that man's problem is sin. One thousand years of a perfect environment, government, health and economy amid world peace will not change man!

The Lord will slay the armies of unbelievers and cast the devil into the lake of fire. He will begin to burn clean the sin cursed universe (2 Pt 3:7-13; Rv 20:11) and will forever judge death and Hades (Rv 20:11-15).

He will resurrect all unbelieving dead and judge their works. This is not to see if they have earned eternal life nor to prove they are lost. It is time for them to confess Christ as Lord (King) and for Him to determine the severity of their eternal punishment.

This is not a judgment for us. Ours will have occurred at the Judgment Seat to determine the extent of our reward and roles in the Lord's realm.

At this point, the Lord has finished destroying the works of the devil (1 Jn 2:8). He and sinners are eternally punished. Sin is removed, death and the place of death are judged and the cursed earth and universe are made new. All enemies of God are gone. Only the righteous remain on earth with the High King.

Phase 2: The Eternal Earthly Kingdom

The Millennium will then merge into the eternal kingdom, what we call heaven. It will be on a new earth in a new universe, precisely as God began in Eden.

The Capital City

Rather than a garden in Eden as God's dwelling and man's capital, heaven will center on the New Jerusalem floating above the new earth (Rv 21:1-27).

The magnificent city that God designed and built (Hb 11:10) will be cube shaped with the length, width and height of almost 1500 miles! The foundation alone will be 2.25 million square miles! That's more living space than everyone who's ever lived would need.[1] It will be the dwelling place for several groups, including you (Hb 12:22-24).

It is not only a beautiful city; it also pictures the values that we must live by now if we intend to reign then. Streets are paved with gold. Priceless jewels are foundation stones. Pearls are gates. All the material things we so crave in this world are construction materials in that one. We who turn our back on this age to invest life in that one will find ourselves greatly rewarded there (Mt 6:19-21; 19:29-30; Jn 12:25-26; Gl 6:6-10; Jn 2:15-17).

Our Eternal Pursuits

This eternally perfect kingdom will be paradise on a new earth in a new heaven, shared by God and man, just as at the beginning, only better. God's sovereignty will be fully vindicated. John describes this restoration in Revelation 22:3-5.

There will no longer be any curse; and the Throne of God and of the Lamb will be in it, and His bond-servants will serve Him (**followership**); *they will see His face, and His name will be on their foreheads* (**fellowship**). *And there will no longer be any night; and they will not have need of the light of a lamp nor the light of the sun, because the Lord God will illumine them; and they will reign forever and ever* (**rulership**).

This trio should guide our life now; they will actually be that life. We will live, work, play, learn, travel and create so that each activity expresses perfect yet growing fellowship, followership and rulership. Ever fulfilled, never bored, continually maturing, relating, improving and celebrating. What a way to live!

Even so, come quickly Lord Jesus!

---

[1] David Jeremiah, *The Prophecy Answer Book* (Nashville, TN: Thomas Nelson, 2010), 166.

Appendix 3

About Rewards

Let's answer some questions about rewards.

What Are Rewards?

Scripture uses numerous terms to describe rewards such as *inheritance, prize, crown*, etc. Two Greek words are chief. *Misthos*—reward—is a wage paid, what we call a paycheck (Mt 20:8; 1 Tm 5:18). It sometimes includes honor as well as a wage for a job well done (Lk 6:20–23).

The other primary word is *apodidomi*, "to repay" or "to reimburse" like the Good Samaritan promised to do (Mt 6:6; Lk 10:35; 14:14).

Christ will reimburse whatever time, effort, money or inconvenience we expend in a good work. Not only that, He will pay us. In the short term, sacrifice and service may cost us very, very much, even life. But they actually cost us nothing in the long run. In fact, they accrue immeasurable profit to our account. Amazing.

But don't be confused. You don't have to go to the mission field or be a pastor or die as a martyr. Do your job with diligence and integrity or speak graciously and encouragingly, or gladly change a diaper for your exhausted wife in the middle of the night. The stuff of life is the seed plot for rewards.

Rewards are for faithful, ordinary believers doing routine things for eternal reasons.

The High King will reimburse and pay us because He knows exactly what it costs to choose eternity over today, to sacrifice or be misunderstood, criticized and rejected because of faithfulness.

Jesus struggled with temptation and persevered in service and suffering until death. One reason He did was for the reward that awaited Him (Hb 12:2). He offers them to us for the same reason. They are real, tangible, useful remuneration graciously bestowed for our loyal obedience, suffering, service and stewardship.

It was commencement the end of my fourth year in college with one to go. My wife and I were both working and planting a church ninety minutes from school. After tuition, gas, food and rent we had almost zero income. I had to take a full load to finish, and we had a baby due just after the next school year started and were uninsured. We had prayed and prayed for God's direction and provision.

While sitting there thinking about all that, they called my name and awarded me a small scholarship for my senior year! Couldn't believe it; even began to cry. Long story short, they summoned me forward five more times that day. God took care of our need through the school's reward system. They had noticed our faithfulness, ministry, grades, etc. and the Spirit led them to reward us. We were just floored!

Just like the scholarships, we will use our rewards to serve in the kingdom. We will be grateful for them and humbled by them. In fact, they will be precious to us because they reflect Gods estimate of our earthly walk with Him and Jesus.

Are Rewards Real or Symbolic?

The kingdom will be much like Eden reborn. Everything there was real, not symbolic or metaphorical. The second Eden will be the same—real relationships, jobs, families, animals, etc. And just as Adam's offspring built cities, pursued commerce and created cultures, so will the last Adam's family.

Rewards will be real too. Some of the descriptions of rewards employ figures of speech, but each describes a real entity. They will consist of genuine treasure, dwellings, crowns, authority and many other concrete and substantial things that will be incorruptible (1 Pt 1:4) and imperishable (1 Cr 9:25).

When Do We Get Rewards?

When do you retire? After many years of labor and regular investing. So it is with rewards; they come after we finish our Christian life, in the next world.

Jesus said, "*. . . you will be repaid at the resurrection of the righteous*" (Lk 14:14b). We receive rewards at our resurrection which will occur at the Rapture. The place and time of our reward is the Judgment Seat that follows the Rapture.

All earthly blessings come from above and are to be enjoyed (1 Tm 6:17), but God's primary intent for them is that we invest them in service and sacrifice so we will enjoy abundant rewards in the next life (1 Tm 6:18-19).

Gaining rewards demands daily diligence, long-term vision, patient endurance and delayed gratification. Our best life now is not His plan for us; living for the present is a losing proposition. We must learn to live with an opposite world value system (Lk 6:20-36; Hb 11:24-26).

Are Rewards Guaranteed?

No. In Matthew 6:1-6, the king warns that when we perform our good works for the wrong reasons we lose the reward. For instance, to pray, fast or give for man's notice is to receive our entire reward when they praise us.

We can also miss rewards or lose our inheritance in other ways. Among these are ongoing laziness or poor stewardship (Lk 19:11-27), persistent evil conduct (Gl 5:19-21), worthless works (1 Cr 3:11-15) and despising our birthright (Hb 12:14-17).[1]

Will Rewards Vary?

When our son finished his first year of soccer at age four, we were stunned. The league presented the same trophy to every player on every team. There was no league champion—everyone was equal. Regardless of faithfulness to practice, effort expended on learning fundamentals or attitudes and team play, each player received the same participation trophy, even those who skipped practice and showed up for only a game or two. The goal was to make everyone feel good about themselves.

Think about that scenario. It redefines participation from effort to signing up. It undermines best effort and esteems mediocrity. Equal reward for all devalues the exertion of those who worked hard to raise their skill level. And in doing that it lessens the significance of the trophy. It is unjust.

Not so in the kingdom. Paul wrote that greater faithfulness earns greater recognition. Consider 2 Timothy 4:6-8.

> *For I am already being poured out as a drink offering, and the time of my departure has come. I have fought the good fight, I have finished the course, I have kept the faith; in the future there is laid up for me the crown of righteousness, which the Lord, the righteous Judge, will*

> *award to me on that day; **and not only to me, but also to all who have loved His appearing.***

Paul anticipates a future crown for two reasons. First, the Lord is *the righteous Judge* who will evaluate justly. Justice will give to each what is due, no more and no less. It would be unrighteous to give an American sister who never once shared Christ the same reward as a witnessing and martyred Chinese sister. Christ will reward rightly because He is righteous.

Second, Paul described loving the Lord's appearing as having *fought the good fight, finished the course* and *kept the faith*. He wrestled with living in light of the kingdom (1 Tm 6:12). He faithfully fulfilled his call to suffer, plant churches and teach the grace of God (Ac 9:10-19; 20:24) and he obeyed until death (1 Tm 6:20; 2 Tm 1:14).

That's what it means to love the Lord's appearing—to live faithfully until death or the Rapture because He is coming. The crown of righteousness awaits those who do. Those who don't will miss it.

Jesus also taught distinctions in reward. See Luke 19:11-27 for one example. Their extent depends on the degree of faithfulness to the opportunities and responsibilities He gives us.

But Don't We Serve as Slaves?

Unquestionably. He is our Master. Service is His due and our duty. Isn't that what Jesus Himself said in Luke 17:10-17?

> *"Which of you, having a slave plowing or tending sheep, will say to him when he has come in from the field, 'Come immediately and sit down to eat'? But will he not say to him, 'Prepare something for me to eat, and properly clothe yourself and serve me while I eat and drink; and afterward you may eat and drink'? He does not thank the slave because he did the things which were commanded, does he? So you too, when you do all the things which are*

> *commanded you, say, 'We are unworthy slaves; we have done only that which we ought to have done.'"*

But just a chapter later in Lk 18:28-30, the King also taught His men to serve to gain reward. This conversation is so meaningful that Matthew 19:27-30, Mark 10:28-31 and Luke record it.

> *Peter said, "Behold, we have left our own homes and followed You" [what then will there be for us? (Mt 19:27)]. And He said to them, "Truly I say to you, there is no one who has left house or wife or brothers or parents or children, for the sake of the kingdom of God, who will not receive many times as much at this time and in the age to come, eternal life."*

Kind Roman masters sometimes paid skilled, faithful slaves for their labors. Our Lord is Lord of all lords and does far better. Serve for obligation's sake but also for remuneration. That's the Master's command and promise.

But We Serve Because We Love Him!

"I love the Lord. I don't need rewards. It makes me feel mercenary." Keep loving! Just remember that to love Him is far more than a feeling; love is an action verb (Jn 14:15, 21). The King said,

> *If **you love Me** you will **keep My commandments** . . . he who has My commandments and **keeps them** is the one **who loves Me** . . .*

Clearly, we love Him by obeying Him. Elsewhere He commanded (not suggested) us to seek rewards and kingdom positions (Mt 6:1-8, 16-24). It follows then that if we love Him, we will pursue them. We are not covetous to be motivated by reward; instead, we are expressing our love to Him. We should feel glad and privileged, not mercenary. It glorifies Him.

Aren't Rewards Self-serving?

"How can you say we ought to seek rewards for ourselves? Didn't Jesus tell us to deny ourselves?" Yes indeed, but He also encouraged the practice of eternal self–interest. In fact, He commanded it too.

He said, *"lay up treasures **for yourselves**." Lay up* is a command rather than a suggestion. In Luke 16:9 His imperative was,

> *"**make friends for yourselves** by means of the wealth of unrighteousness, **so that** when it fails, **they will receive you** into the eternal dwellings."*

There is a distinction between selfish (what I do harms others — there is only one parachute on the plane and I take it to your demise) and self—interest (there are parachutes for all and I take one for my preservation).[2] The Lord Jesus insists on kingdom self–interest as godly motivation.

He also taught the Twelve (and us) to pursue eternal ambition and seek kingdom greatness (Mk 10:35-45). Remember this conversation?

> *James and John, the two sons of Zebedee, came up to Jesus, saying, "Teacher, we want You to do for us whatever we ask of You." And He said to them, "What do you want Me to do for you?" They said to Him, "Grant that we may sit, one on Your right and one on Your left, in Your glory."*
>
> *Hearing this, the ten began to feel indignant with James and John. Calling them to Himself, Jesus said to them, "You know that those who are recognized as rulers of the Gentiles lord it over them; and their great men exercise authority over them. But it is not this way among you, but **whoever wishes to become great among you** shall be your servant; and **whoever wishes to be first***

among you shall be slave of all. For even the Son of Man did not come to be served, but to serve, and to give His life a ransom for many."

Jesus did not correct their "bad theology" or "corrupt desires" for wanting high kingdom positions. Instead, He told them how to be great in the world to come: be a humble, proactive servant to all men in this one!

You see, the Lord wants us to be as high as possible in the kingdom for it glorifies Him. Eternal ambition is smart, not selfish; it is spiritual, not sinful. Jesus commands it. Pursue it.

How Do We Gain Rewards?

While writing this section I attended the funeral of a former professor, father figure, friend, advisor and employer. He was a very human and godly man, and the rich celebration of his life and home–going lasted over two hours.

After decades as a powerful husband, father, grandfather, preacher, teacher, evangelist, leader and mentor, cancer consumed his last several years. But he never quit serving. He turned his active public ministry of the Word into the private ministry of worship and intercession four hours a day. He prayed for hundreds of missionaries day after day, week after week, year after year. He finished well.

In a nutshell that's how we gain rewards. We see and seek the King and His kingdom until the end (2 Tm 4:6-8; Hb 11:6-16, 24-26).

Scripture doesn't give a list of what Jesus will reward. Usually when you find a recompense mentioned, the actions for it are right there in the verse or immediate context. However, you will see many things repeated along with the idea of faithfulness, diligence or perseverance through trials. Here are some lifestyle acts and attitudes that we can all do until our end.

- Secret acts of prayer, fasting and giving to the poor (Mt 6:6-8, 16-18)
- Endure suffering for following Christ (Mt 5:11-12; Lk 6:22-23)
- Deny your independent plans and desires daily and submit to Christ, even unto death (Mt 16:24-27)
- Leave possessions and family to follow Christ and make Him known (Mt 19:27-30)
- Do the little things for fellow brothers and servants of Christ (Mk 9:4; Hb 6:12)
- Help those who are in need (Mk 9:41)
- Love your enemies and do good to them (Lk 6:35)
- Witness consistently (2 Cr 5:9-11)
- Serve and lead at work as if employed by Christ (Co 3:22-24)
- Invest your money and possessions in eternal purposes (1 Tm 6:17-19)

There are many, many others, but these clearly show that any saint can do them. Nothing says we must be perfect, a missionary or a martyr; just adjust our worldview to that of Jesus and keep after it. That's what happens when we seek first the kingdom of God and His righteousness.

What Are the Rewards?

We can summarize rewards in at least five broad categories.

Rewards Include People

Disciples who use their material resources to forward the gospel will enjoy enriched relationships with those their investments impacted. In eternity, they will welcome us into their homes with particular joy and fellowship (Lk 16:9)! Those who share Christ with the lost and promote believers' growth will connect with them and intensely celebrate them forever (1 Th 2:19-20).

Imagine walking down a street in New Jerusalem when you hear in accented English, "Hey, Marcia!" You turn to look and there is a woman you've never met. She walks up smiling and says, "I've got your favorite meal on the table inside. It would be such a privilege if we could spend a few years together. We can tell each other stories about our earthly lives following Jesus."

With arm extended to hug her you respond, "Well, sure! I'd love to. What's your name?" She steps inside your arm to squeeze you back with, "I'm Yesika from the Nagi people in interior Papua. We've never met, but I know you. You and your husband Bill prayed and invested to send Porter and Lexi Hampton and their children to my tribe. After a long time, I believed in Jesus and put away the dead, liar gods."

"No way!" you cry.

"Yes way, as you Americans say! Come on, let's eat and let me and my Nagi brothers and sisters celebrate you. Porter and Lexi are here as well as Paul and Joan who led their mission group. And so is Rob. He discipled Porter and Lexi. Now you can really catch up with all of us and we can say a proper Nagi thank you!" "Oh, can we get Bill? He'll want in on this!" "Sure, let me send an angel for him."

Every Bill and Marcia, Rob, Porter and Lexi and Paul and Joan who invested in the Nagi's life and growth will have more intimate relations with them forever. Exquisite.

Just as with all other rewards, today is the time to prepare those relationships. Of course, when we think of people, the Father Himself is paramount. We will grow in our relational knowledge of the Father and Son for eternity (Jn 17:3). Since He is eternal and made us for fellowship, we will ever be connecting more deeply with Him. Those who cultivate more intimacy with God in this life will know Him better in the next life (Jn 14:18-24; Rv 21:7; 22:3-4). God Himself will be our greatest bonus!

Rewards Include Position

Man is made to rule the earth. It seems that every believer will govern to some degree because God does not fail at whatever He intends. We are a kingdom of priests which includes rule of some sort (Rv 1:6; 5:10). Every church age believer is part of the bride who will be the queen of the new earth, which demands we all rule (Rv 19:7-8). Perhaps all saints will have at least one angel to rule in some way. *Judge* seems to include legal decision-making or oversight (1 Cr 6:1-3).

However, if we all rule, our authority will vary. The very least may rule an angel. Others will govern and steward cities, states, even nations. The King will assign different spheres of authority and responsibility based on our stewardship (Lk 19:17-19; Rv 2:26-27).

Perhaps you think, "The last thing I want to do is be a bureaucrat forever. That's so unappealing." Ah, but there's a difference. There it will be incomparable joy, driven by love and grace, leading perfect people rather than sinners. You won't even be able to not enjoy it! And it won't be all you do in the kingdom, not even close. Life will be more filled with pleasure than we can ever imagine.

Note what Jesus taught in a parable about faithful stewardship. He judges, addresses and rewards three different servants.

> *And he said to him [the first], "Well done, good slave, because you have been faithful in a very little thing, you are to be in authority over ten cities." (Lk 19:17)*
>
> *And he said to him [the second] also, "And you are to be over five cities." (Lk 19:19)*
>
> *He said to him [the third], "By your own words I will judge you, you worthless slave. . ." Then he said to the*

> bystanders, *"Take the mina away from him and give it to the one who has the ten minas."* (Lk 19:22, 24)

The Lord honored the first with, *"Well done, good slave."* He gave no commendation to the second and described the last as *worthless!* Only some will hear the King's exhilarating, "Well done!" Bu how devastating should the King call us worthless for His use.

When it was all said and done, the first slave held authority over ten cities, the second over five and the useless third none. If all believers rule, only steadfast stewards will exercise great eternal power.

Rewards Include Possessions

There will be commerce in the kingdom (Rv 21:24-26) so we will need assets (Mt 6:19-21). This life is our only opportunity to make financial preparation for the life to come. Therefore, the King commands us to lay up treasure in heaven (Mt 6:19-24; 1 Tm 6:17-19). Giving is genuinely investing in the one place where there is no chance of loss, no risk on return and failsafe ROI. The Lord Himself is the guarantee of everlasting return.

Jesus also promises eternal physical belongings to those who leave present possessions for the gospel's sake (Mt 19:29-30). What we sacrifice and send ahead in service to others He will graciously reimburse and multiply, and we will always possess and enjoy them (Lk 14:12-14).

Remarkably, investing money and material goods for reward may be the one act over which we have the most control, other than private prayer.

And remember, if we are poor or low income now, that does not prohibit us from investing very well indeed. One day the King sat and observed the givers in the temple treasury. Listen to His lesson in Mark 14:41-44.

> *And He sat down opposite the treasury and began observing how the people were putting money into the treasury; and many rich people were putting in large sums. A poor widow came and put in two small copper coins, which amount to a cent. Calling His disciples to Him, He said to them,* **"Truly I say to you, this poor widow put in more than all the contributors to the treasury; for they all put in out of their surplus, but she, out of her poverty, put in all she owned, all she had to live on."**

The pitiable widow withheld nothing. She gave *all she had to live on*. Her offering left her without recourse for widows had no social security, rare prospects for work, no fall back. Many today could give 100% of their next paycheck and never miss a beat. But she would miss her next meal.

Her sacrifice is unimaginable to us. We would likely criticize her for poor stewardship. But Jesus commended her. Perhaps most remarkable is that it put her in a place where she only had one hope of provision—trusting the God whom she so richly loved to care for her. He was sitting right there watching. I think He did.

What made her gift so valuable? Its amount, the sacrifice it entailed, the faith exercised and the motive behind it.

By the way, did you note that the Lord sees the amount as very important? That's why the gift of a penny can be worth more than a billion and why the poor can out give the wealthy. He measures the amount of our offering by the size of the sacrifice.

Don't you think her reward for that act of worship will be grand? No telling what her return will be. I look forward to celebrating her on that day.

Rewards Include Prestige

Some rewards deal with relational, physical and emotional pleasures and prestige. You might shine brighter than others as you reflect God's glory (Dn 12:2-3). You may be the focus of a special celebration when you enter the kingdom (2 Pt 1:10-11)! And you might wear a crown or two with the gratification that will bring.

The ancient world knew two types of crown. One belonged to kings—a sovereign crown. The other was the victors crown for those who won athletic contests.

Scripture mentions five victor's crowns as rewards for faithfulness in specific areas. They include the crown of life (Jm 1:12), the crown of glory (1 Pt 5:1-4) and the crown of righteousness (2 Tm 4:6-8). There is also the crown of rejoicing (1 Th 2:19) and the incorruptible crown (1 Cr 9:24-25).

In New Testament times, the winners crown gave the person fame, wealth and freedom from taxes. This is the kind of pleasure and honor that crowns will bring those who earn them.

Rewards Include Privilege

Some servants, even some churches, will receive distinct rewards. To each of the seven churches in Revelation 2-3 Jesus promises unique pleasures to those referred to as *overcomers*. Depending on how you define overcomer, you can say that all believers receive them or only those who fulfill the requirements. It seems to me that all believers are overcomers by position (1 Jn 2:13-14; 5:4-5) but only some overcome in practice (Rv 2-3).

Overcomers will receive highly valuable, special privileges and positions in the kingdom. Many of these rewards are literal while others seem to be litotes, (you won't be sorry, meaning you'll be glad). Whatever these rewards are, they are a very rare class.

Another privilege available is a distinct resurrection, an "out-resurrection" group singled out from all resurrected ones (Ph 3:12). Theirs is *a better resurrection* (Hb 11:35). They are worthy of that distinction because they strove for a greater fellowship with Christ, endured tremendous suffering and lived for the kingdom and its rewards (Ph 3:10-14).

Finally, there is the privilege of companionship or partnership with Christ. Hebrews is about pursuing this reward by faith in His kingdom promises. Pursuit includes obedient living, enduring suffering and steadfast participation in corporate prayer, witness and encouragement. It seems that His companions may be a unique, intimate ruling council. They will know Him better, rejoice with Him more and work with Him more closely to implement His plans. Luke uses the same term to describe the disciples as business partners (5:7).

Rewards Include Praise

To some believers the King will say, *"Well done good and faithful servant."* He will confess to the Father and His angels the faithfulness of those who acknowledge Him and witness to others (Mt 10:32; Lk 12:8). Can you imagine hearing such words from the Lord Jesus Christ? What an unspeakable opportunity rewards give us!

To read that power, possessions or pleasure are available forever may sound unspiritual. It's not. Remember that God made us to enjoy people, possessions and pleasure and to exercise infinite power over the earth. And as David wrote, *In Your presence is fullness of joy; in Your right hand there are pleasures forever* (Ps 16:11).[3]

According to Jesus, everything is right about wanting to have and enjoy such blessings—except where and how we work so hard to fulfill them. It is not so much that our desires are wrong but that we try to satisfy them via the present world that is passing away and competes with our love for God.

Your heavenly Father wants to reward His children. Your King wants to reward His servants. Let's make them happy.

---

[1] Ray Baughman, *The Kingdom of God Visualized* (Chicago: Moody Press, 1972), 211–15.

[2] Dr. Bill Korver, President of Carolina College of Biblical Studies shared this illustration with me. He heard Zane Hodges use it at a Grace Evangelical Society conference, date unknown.

[3] Randy Alcorn, *The Law of Rewards* (Wheaton, IL: Tyndale House Publishers, Inc., 2003), 111–121.

Appendix 4

The Inheritance

The biblical inheritance differs from that in our culture. Believing Old Testament Israelites have two inheritances. The first is God Himself; they are His and He is theirs forever (Gn 17:7; Ps 16:5; 73:25-26; 119:57; 142:5). Personal fellowship with God in time and eternity is an absolute grace gift to every Old Testament believer.

Believing Israel's second inheritance is the eternal occupation of Canaan. Persons sometimes own beachfront properties they only visit for a couple of weeks every year or so. Likewise, Israel possesses (owns) the land legally but does not yet possess (fully occupy or inherit) it experientially.

Their full inheritance of the land is conditional. It is a reward in the millennium to be gained by obedience, faith and completed conflict (Dt 6:18-19; 11:22-25; 15:4-5; 19:14; 25:17-26:2).

Thus, the Hebrew Scriptures often designate full occupation of the land and freedom from all enemies as *rest*. As it is conditional, inheriting rest can be forfeited by disbelief and disobedience (Nm 14; Dt 4:21-22).

In summary, all believing Israelites own the land forever although individual Israelite believers may or may not occupy it in the kingdom. That will be a reward for their enduring faithfulness.

Believers in Jesus also have two inheritances. Like Israel, God Himself is our first birthright, solely by grace through faith in Jesus.

As positional *heirs of God* we can enjoy Him right now and forever (Rm 8:17; Ti 3:4-7). This inheritance is *imperishable, undefiled and will not fade away* because God keeps it for us (1 Pt 1:3-5).

Heirs of God

It is staggering what being God's heir includes. Here's a list from just one passage, Galatians 3:23-4:7.

- Freedom from the Law. It is not your rule of life (3:23-25).
- Justification. God has declared you legally righteous (3:24).
- Adoption. You are God's adult son and legal heir (3:26; 4:1-7).
- Union with Christ. God sees you as He does His Son (3:27-28).
- Abraham's descendant. You are His spiritual child by faith in Christ and a legal heir of the promise (3:29; cf. 4:7).
- Liberty from the elements. Not religion but relationship with God (4:3).
- Redemption. Jesus freed you from sin and will resurrect you (4:4-5).
- The Holy Spirit lives within to empower and guide you (4:6).
- Intimacy with our Father. He enjoys time with you (4:6).
- Heir through God. A legal heir to the kingdom (4:7)

That is amazing grace, is it not?

As incredible as it is, there is a second inheritance. Being an heir of God deals primarily with our personal fellowship with Him. The other focuses on our eternal functions.

Heirs of the Kingdom

Our second inheritance is to *inherit the kingdom*. This does not mean to get saved. It is future possession of the rewards and roles we will fully enjoy in the kingdom (Co 3:24; Rm 8:17b, et al.).

An Heir of God	An Heir of the Kingdom
Free gift by grace through faith	Rewards for faith and works
Received at belief in Jesus	Received at the Judgment Seat
Unconditional	Conditional

Our inheritance is obtained by works, awarded at the Judgment Seat of Christ and can be missed.

God wants us to attain it, so He has given everything we need *for life and godliness* (2 Pt 1:3). Below are some ways to *inherit the kingdom*.

Some Ways to Gain Kingdom Inheritance		
Passage	Condition	Inheritance
Lk 12:8; 19:17	Faithful witness	Verbal praise
Lk 19:17, 19	Eternal use of money	Rule of cities
Rm 8:17b	Suffer with Christ	Co-rule with Christ
1 Tm 6:19	Eternal investing	Financial foundation
Hb 11:35	Suffer to death	Better resurrection
Jm 1:12, etc.	Enduring faithfulness	Victor's crowns
2 Pt 1:5-11	Diligent character growth	Celebrated kingdom entrance
Rv 2-3	Overcome special challenges	Overcomer rewards

The Lord has also mentioned several ways to lose inheritance so we can avoid doing so. Should we lose it, we lose it forever.

Some Ways to Lose Kingdom Inheritance		
Passage	Phrase	Cause
1 Cr 6:9-11	...will not inherit the kingdom	Sinful character and practices
Gl 5:19-21	...will not inherit the kingdom	Sinful character and practices
Ep 5:3-5	No... inheritance	Sinful character and practices
Hb 4:1	Not enter His rest	An evil, disbelieving heart
Hb 6:8	Close to being cursed	Regressing from growth
Hb 10:36	You need endurancce	Abandoning priestly roles
Hb 12:25	How much less will we escape	Refuse Him who is speaking

We gain much in eternity for faithfulness today. Let's press on to receive the reward of the inheritance.

Appendix 5

Jesus and Temptation

Jesus is God and God can't sin, so how could He really be tempted?

> *... He Himself was tempted in that which He has suffered ... He [has] been tempted in all things as we are, yet without sin.* (Hb 2:18; 4:15)

> According to Matthew, *Jesus was led up by the Spirit into the wilderness to be tempted by the devil.* (4:1)

> Luke agrees, recording that *Jesus . . .was led around by the Spirit in the wilderness for forty days, being tempted by the devil.* (4:1-2a)

Let's try to glean some helpful answers to how this can be.

Jesus Was Fully Human and Temptable

In the beginning, Adam was the head of the new human race. He was a perfect reflection of God with no sin nature, for sin is not a natural part of humanity.

Christ is the second Adam, the perfect image of God with no sin nature (2 Cr 4:4), and head of the second new race (Rm 5:12-21; 1 Cr 15:20-28, 42-49).

Neither Adam nor Jesus were tempted by an inward desire for sin. Though neither had a sin nature, their humanity was totally temptable from without.

Jesus Was Fully Tempted and Resisted

When tempted, Adam chose to sin knowing full well what he was doing (1 Tm 2:13-14). When he failed the test, he lost spiritual life and the kingdom. To restore the fallen race and realm, the man Jesus had to be tempted and pass the test.

To succeed where Adam failed, Jesus was tempted in His humanity only, not His deity. God cannot be tempted (Jm 1:13) and man must regain rule (Ps 8; Hb 2:5-18). Indeed, every time Scripture mentions Him by name regarding His temptations, it uses Jesus, His human name.

Sometimes Jesus the God–Man limited the free use of some aspect of His deity to operate within human limitations (Mt 24:36; Jn 4:6; 19:28). He did not give up deity; He limited its independent exercise. It seems He did that in His temptations.

Jesus was tempted forty days, not just three times on the last day (Lk 4:2). He had to say, "No" many more than three times. Indeed, He was tempted throughout His ministry (Lk 4:13; Mt 16:23; 27:35-44) and He passed every test without sin. Since He endured every temptation successfully, He experienced such tests more thoroughly than we do when we yield to them.

Jesus felt these pressures even more intensely because His emotions, mind and nerves were unhindered by sin. A child's tender hand is far more sensitive to a needle prick than a carpenter's calloused palm.

When Satan challenged, *if you are the Son of God* (Gk. and you are) he did not question Jesus' deity or try to make Him doubt Himself. He tempted Jesus to depend on Himself as Son of God rather than as a man depending on God. The examination was independence versus dependence and Jesus passed.

The original temptation was the same. The serpent offered autonomy—the knowledge of good and evil like God if they ate from the fruit of the tree and Adam went for it. He yielded to the one temptation because he depended on himself and followed Eve's word rather than trusting God and obeying His word. Adam's failure was independence over dependence.

Jesus' Temptations Worked for Him

And having been made perfect, He became to all those who obey Him the source of eternal salvation . . . (Hb 5:9).

Before His incarnation, Jesus did not experientially know what it was like for a human to walk with God in a wayward world. But His temptations perfected His humanity so that He now understands by participation the trials and pressures of obeying God.

He resisted the enticements and demonstrated the righteousness necessary to rule the kingdom. In this way He became qualified to serve as our sinless savior (2 Cr 5:21; Hb 4:15; 1 Pt 2:22; 3:18; 1 Jn 3:5), sovereign king (Hb 1:8-9), empathetic high priest (Hb 4:15), righteous advocate (1 Jn 2:1) and sovereign Lord (Mt 28:18).

Jesus' Temptations Worked for Us

For we do not have a high priest who cannot sympathize with our weaknesses, but One who has been tempted in all things as we are, yet without sin. (Hb 4:14-16).

Our *weaknesses* in these verses are our susceptibilities to all the pains and challenges of human experience and their impact on our spiritual life. Independence, ridicule, betrayal, unrequited love, the grief of loss, suffering, discouragement and tiredness, addiction to power or pleasure—this is being human. These affect our choices as Christians. Our tests can turn into temptation and our temptation into sin because we are weak.

All that He gained through resisting temptation, we profit from. Jesus is our victorious savior who delivers us from sin, both now and forever. Tested and true, He has regained the kingdom and prepares us for it. He is our empathetic, empowering high priest who gives mercy and grace when we cry out to Him. He is our righteous advocate who restores our fellowship and our sovereign authority for witness and spiritual warfare.

The Lord is also our model of resisting temptation. He demonstrated a determination to obey the Father. A kingdom view of the present world. Memorization of the Scripture. Speaking that word aloud when needed. Trusting God for the strength to press on.

As with salvation, the kingdom, inheritance and rewards, the Lord's temptations are central to God's purpose of vindicating His sovereignty and restoring His image in man.

Note the comparisons and contrasts below.

The Temptation of the Two Kings	
Adam	Jesus
God's son (Lk 3:38)	God's Son
Perfect human	Perfect human
Was King of the Earth	Will be King of the Earth
Ruled with his bride	Will rule with His bride
His bride led him into temptation	The Spirit led Him into temptation
Tempted when accompanied	Tempted when alone
At the peak of physical health	At the depth of physical weakness
Fully fed	Hungry & thirsty after 40 days' fast
Knew God's one word of law	Knew God's complete law
Satan's 1st use of temptation	Satan after 4,000+ years of practice
Tempted externally	Tempted externally
Tempted secondarily, after Eve	Tempted primarily, face-to-face
Was silent when tempted	Spoke the Scripture when tempted
Yielded to one temptation	Refused 40 + days of temptation
Brought sin and death to all	Brought justification & life to many
Satan left him	Satan left Him for a time
Gave away kingdom authority	Recaptured kingdom authority
Gn 3; 1 Cr 15; Rm 5	Mt 1, 4; Lk 1-2, 4; Hb 2, 4

Jesus was truly and fully tempted and resisted them all.

Appendix 6

The Judgment Seat

The New Testament mentions or implies the Judgment Seat of Christ over 75 times. Let's overview of some of what it reveals.

What the Judgment Seat Is
It Is a Place
A Judgment Seat (Gk. bema) was a seat on a raised platform in a city marketplace. There, governors and judges handed down legal decisions and awarded winning athletes (Jn 19:13; Ac 18:12). Christ's bema will be in the heavenlies. He will publicly distribute any rewards and assign us our kingdom roles after He evaluates us.

It Is an Event
Broadly speaking, in the Christian life we function as *sons*, *slaves*, *stewards* and *priests*. Christ will judge the quality of our works in these arenas. *Son* deals with our relationship to our Father, our elder Brother and to one another. *Slaves* must obey, while *stewardship* covers all the opportunities and responsibilities we

receive. As *priests*, we have responsibilities to the Trinity and the body of Christ.

Jesus will evaluate our Christian life from the instant of belief in Him to death or the Rapture. Nothing before believing in Him will come up. There will be no judgment of sins as we legally have none to judge. The cross cancelled those charges forever.

Consequences of our sins as believers will affect the extent of our rewards. They change the opportunities and quality of our present service and relationships. However, they will not be judged as sins.

When the Judgment Seat Occurs

All future judgments occur after a resurrection. Ours will happen after the Rapture (Lk 14:14). The analysis of the Old Testament and Tribulation saints will take place shortly after the Second Coming (Dn 12:1-3, 11-13). Christ will raise all unbelievers to face Him at the Great White Throne after the Millennium (Rv 20:7-15).

Who the Judge Will Be

The exalted Lord Jesus will be our Judge as the Father has entrusted all judgment to Him (Jn 5:22-23, 25-27). As God-Man He will know all mitigating circumstances, opportunities, abilities, etc. by experience and intellect. He will be perfectly righteous and just.

Why We Go to the Judgment Seat

> *For we must all appear before the Judgment Seat of Christ, so that each one may be recompensed for his deeds in the body, according to what he has done, whether good or bad.* (2 Cr 5:10)

To Reveal Our Motives

There are several reasons for our assessment. *We must all **appear*** indicates far more than just make an appearance. He will make transparent our hidden works and motives (Lk 12:2-3; 1 Cr 4:5; Hb 4:12).

Everything we have ever done and said as believers will be publicly revealed. This exposure will determine the eternal value of our works and the extent of our rewards.

We probably never have singular motives, nor is this necessarily bad. Jesus did things for many reasons. Among others, they include the joy of reward to come (Hb 12:1-2) and love of the Father (Jn 14:31). He acted because the Bible said to (Mt 4:1-11), because He loved righteousness (Hb 1:9) and to express compassion (Mk 1:41).

It is the nature of our stimuli, not the number, that is the issue: dark versus light, eternal versus temporal and God's kingdom versus our own.

Acceptable motivations include our love for Christ and others. Gratitude for grace and mercy are also suitable. Healthy reasons embrace the sense of accountability and responsibility and to gain rewards. Remarkably, it appears that rewards are the most commonly used incentive in the Bible for obedience and service!

All these motivations glorify God.

To Rectify Relationships Between Brothers

The Lord will correct or vindicate that which is unjust or inequitable in our relationships. It is easy for others to misunderstand or judge us and vice versa.

> *But you, why do you **judge your brother**? Or you again, why do you **regard your brother with contempt**? For we will all stand before **the Judgment Seat** of God.* (Rm 14:10)

Sins such as partiality or lack of mercy harm and hinder others. Prejudice, social standing, power, even age make it easy to take advantage of others and for brothers to look down upon one another. The Lord will square away such things once and forever (Jm 2:1-13; 5:1-11).

To Reveal the Quality of Our Ministry Materials

First Corinthians 3:10-15 speaks directly to spiritual leaders such as church planters, missionaries, pastors and elders–servants who establish and build the local church, *God's building*. They will answer for greater privilege and responsibility.

Teachers will face stricter judgment (Jm 3:1), and there will be a special reward for faithful elders (1 Pt 5:4). It seems natural that the Lord will look for similar essential traits in all His people since all believers are to serve and build the church.

He will evaluate the authority for ministry that we used—how well we proclaimed, followed and focused on Jesus Christ and Scripture—*the wisdom of God* (1 Cr 1:18–3:4). We can live by two authorities: the wisdom of God in Scripture or the wisdom of the world in the culture, secular or Christian.

Another is the lasting quality of our materials. The *foundation* given to every believer and church is Christ. The believer builds himself and others on that foundation and has a choice of construction materials—eternal and imperishable or temporal and perishable. The Lord will test their real value with fire. Perishable materials include *wood, hay* and *straw*.

> The combustible materials . . . are works that arose out of human "wisdom" in all its forms. These made no lasting contribution, although they may have served some temporary need.[1]

Enduring materials such as *gold, silver* and *precious stones* include the Scripture, love, prayer, personal equipping and mutual care.

To Recompense Our Works

> *We must all appear before the Judgment Seat of Christ so that each one may be recompensed for his deeds in the*

> *body, according to what he has done, whether good or bad.*
> (2 Cr 5:10)

Recompensed carries the idea of receiving what is due or to be paid back (Mt 25:27), so the divine response to our works includes both gain and loss of rewards. The *good* things are those done with proper motives and materials.

Many rewards for good works are available, such as assorted crowns (1 Cr 9:25; 2 Tm 4:8; Jm 1:12, etc.) and diverse roles and opportunities to serve Jesus and others (Mt 25:14-30; Lk 19:11-27). Some will even share Christ's rule (Rv 2:26-27). Our compensation will differ from one another forever because we have diverse opportunities, challenges, abilities and circumstances. Our Judge will repay us perfectly.

There is disagreement over the meaning of the Greek word translated as *bad* (Gk. kakon, or phaulon in some manuscripts). Some translate this kakon as "worthless." Worthless deeds would be unacceptable like incorrectly cut or twisted studs when framing a house. Unusable, they are burned up.[2]

This may be correct, but it appears that it may include more than worthlessness.

> "The word *kakon* always means bad or evil in the New Testament and *phaulon* always means bad or evil when it is contrasted with the word 'good' (*agathos*) as it is here in 2 Corinthians 5:10."[3]

Either way, repayment for bad or evil will include lessened mercy from Christ, denial by Christ, rebuke from Him, or shame before Him, as well as the incineration of the work and the loss of reward.

John warns us that we can be ashamed before Him at His coming (1 Jn 2:28-29). In one parable Jesus severely criticized an unfaithful servant then took away his kingdom stewardship (Lk 19:22). If we have denied Christ, He will in some way deny us, perhaps with a criticism akin to the previous (2 Tm 2:12).

We would all agree that we will crave mercy there. We know how inconsistent we are. Paul wishes mercy on a very faithful servant when he stands for examination (2 Tm 1:18). Even the best servants will need compassion at the bema.

James writes an intriguing, frightening and encouraging word about mercy in 2:12-13. Lack of mercy shown in partiality, indifference or cruelty to other brothers will bring *merciless judgment*. Amazingly, the one who extends much mercy today will receive much compassion on that day. "Mercy triumphs over judgment!"[4]

Other passages teach these same three lessons. We will gain and lose reward; we can be chastised and verbally rebuked and we will need mercy. It is the Judgment Seat, not the reward seat.

How might we respond to the reality of the bema?

Some Responses to the Judgment Seat

- Walk closely with the Lord
- Allow the Bible and the kingdom to frame your worldview and values
- Remind yourself regularly of the coming Judgment Seat
- Believe that your present behavior is causal to your eternal "standard of living"
- Live righteously
- Consistently share the gospel
- Serve faithfully and regularly through your local church
- Work to maintain as peaceful relationships as you can

Finally, remember Jesus' promise:

> *If anyone serves Me, he must follow Me; and where I am, there My servant will be also;* ***if anyone serves Me, the Father will honor him****.* (Jn 12:26)

[1] Thomas L. Constable, "Notes on 1 Corinthians" (2015): 39.
[2] This illustration created by Bill Korver in a conversation with the author. n.d.
[3] Paul N. Benware, *The Believer's Payday* (Chattanooga, TN: AMG Publishers, 2002), 92.
[4] Zane C. Hodges, "Hebrews," in *The Bible Knowledge Commentary*, New Testament. (Wheaton: Victor Books, 1983), 824.

Appendix 7

Chastening and Pruning

In John 15 Jesus likens some of the Father's work in believers to a vinedresser's work on branches. Part of that effort is pruning fruitful branches to increase their fruitfulness. No fruit bearing believer is exempt from this uncomfortable, though critical, process.

Pruning apparently parallels the discipline process in Hebrews 12:9-14. The Vinedresser's purpose is loving, but the process is painful. So it is with the Father and discipline.[1]

This is not to dismiss chastening or punishment for sin as part of God's discipline. It is to emphasize that discipline does not always occur for sin. Its primary goal is training sons for kingdom roles by making them Christlike in character, conduct and worldview. Therefore, it is important to realize that problems, trials and ongoing difficulties are not necessarily indications of God's chastening. They are part of the disciplines of the normal Christian life.

New Testament usage reveals several ways God trains and chastens us.

Different Ways God Disciplines His Sons		
The Means	**The Goal**	**Text**
Instruction	Train for future role	Ac 7:22; 22:3
Weakness, illness, death	Encourage self-judgment	1 Cr 11:27-33
Gentle care, admonition	Bring to adulthood	Ep 6:4
Teaching of the Word	Repentance and purity	2 Tm 2:25; Ti 2:15
Applying the Word	Prepare for ministry	2 Tm 3:16-17
Focus on the grace of the incarnation	Responsible purity	Ti 2:11-12; Ep 4:20-24
Wait for the Rapture	Responsible purity	Ti 2:13
Apply freedom from sin's power	Responsible purity	Ti 2:14
Trials and suffering	Create fortitude & purity	Hb 12:4-7; 1 Pt 5:10
Rebuke from the Word, the Spirit or a brother	Endurance, maturity and fruitfulness	Hb 12:5
Persecution, suffering	Endurance, maturity and fruitfulness	Hb 12:6-14

In summary, discipline is the Father training His sons for maturity and future roles in the kingdom. It includes both chastening for sin and development of character and fruitfulness. It is much like pruning in that both are from the Father, involve pain and aim for greater fruitfulness.

Note the comparisons below.

Comparison of Pruning and Chastening	
John 15:1-11	**Hebrews 12:4-11**
Context is corporate—plurals	Context is corporate—plurals
Context persecution (15:18ff; 16:1ff)	Context is persecution (3-4)
The Father prunes branches (1-2)	The Father disciplines sons (5-6)
Every branch is involved (2)	Every son is involved (6-8)
The Word is involved (3, 7, 10, 11)	The Word is involved (5-6)
The Father's love is stressed (9-10)	The Father's love is stressed (6)
The purpose is bear much fruit (8)	The purpose is fruitfulness (10-11)

---

[1] This topic and similar table introduced to the author in Hebrews class by Dr. James Raiford at Southeastern Bible College, Birmingham, AL in 1979.

Made in the USA
Lexington, KY
03 November 2019